Praise for

The Rhythm of the Christian Life

"Everyone would benefit from pausing to think deeply about the rhythm of their daily life. Wright's book draws from the deep well of Bonhoeffer's work on the rhythm of life; it's refreshing and challenging at the same time. Read it together with someone or schedule it for the end of the year or season. We highly recommend this excellent book."

—**Dave Furman,** Senior Pastor, Redeemer Church of Dubai, and author of *Kiss the Wave* and *Being There*; and his wife, **Gloria Furman,** author of *Labor with Hope* and *Missional Motherhood*

"How best to spend our limited time on earth is arguably our greatest challenge. God instructed Adam to keep the garden, Israel to keep the Sabbath, and the church to keep the feast— all examples of how the people of God are to 'keep time.' *The Rhythm of the Christian Life* explains that keeping time is our most important and neglected spiritual discipline. Only when we coordinate spending time alone with God and together before God will we get our out-of-sync lives back in sync. Forget about the program—get with the beat, the two-beat rhythm of the Christian life that structures Christian freedom and sustains human flourishing."

—**Kevin J. Vanhoozer,** Research Professor of Systematic Theology, Trinity Evangelical Divinity School

"For a long time, I've been looking for a book that is spiritually and intellectually satisfying yet simple. This book does just that. With incredible simplicity, *The Rhythm of the Christian Life* engaged my mind, warmed my heart, and inspired me to apply its message."

—**Maher Samuel,** psychiatrist, apologist, and former Director of Ravi Zacharias International Ministries (RZIM) in the Middle East

"God designed life to be lived together. The wisdom to live, the joy to celebrate, and the love to share are all found and experienced when we live together in harmony. Brian Wright makes this evident for us in the middle of an individualistic generation. Despite our busy schedules, we must find time to spend with God if we want to experience the joy of life together as part of the rhythm of the Christian life. Indeed, the good life is rhythmic. Don't just read this book—live it!"

—**Miguel Núñez,** Senior Pastor, Iglesia Bautista Internacional in Santo Domingo, Dominican Republic, and council member of The Gospel Coalition

"In the hectic, disjointed world, Brian Wright speaks wisdom. His calm measured voice rings as clear as the bell of a watchtower, calling us back to the rhythm of the Christian life. He reminds us that just as inhaling and exhaling are both essential to breathing, so time alone with God and time in fellowship with God's people are equally essential. Building upon the work of Dietrich Bonhoeffer, Wright reminds us that this divine tempo is timeless and universal; God wired us to live this way and he built us to do it in community. Sin disrupts this cadence, and we must deliberately return to the fellowship of God's people, to time alone with God, and again to the cadence of God's rhythm."

—**E. Randolph Richards,** Provost and Chief Academic Officer, Palm Beach Atlantic University, and author of *Misreading Scripture with Western Eyes*

THE
RHYTHM
OF THE
CHRISTIAN
LIFE

Recapturing the Joy of Life Together

BRIAN J. WRIGHT

LEAFWOOD
PUBLISHERS
an imprint of Abilene Christian University Press

THE RHYTHM OF THE CHRISTIAN LIFE
Recapturing the Joy of Life Together

LEAFWOOD
P U B L I S H E R S
an imprint of Abilene Christian University Press

Copyright © 2019 by Brian J. Wright

ISBN 978-1-68426-350-9 | LCCN 2019010990

Printed in the United States of America

LIBRARY OF CONGRESS CATALOGING-IN-PUBLICATION DATA
Names: Wright, Brian J., 1978- author.
Title: The rhythm of the Christian life : recapturing the joy of life
    together / Brian J. Wright.
Description: Abilene, Texas : Leafwood Publishers, 2019.
Identifiers: LCCN 2019010990 | ISBN 9781684263509 (pbk.)
Subjects: LCSH: Christian life.
Classification: LCC BV4501.3 .W737 2019 | DDC 248.4—dc23
LC record available at https://lccn.loc.gov/2019010990

Cover design by ThinkPen Design
Interior text design by Sandy Armstrong, Strong Design

Leafwood Publishers is an imprint of Abilene Christian University Press
ACU Box 29138 | Abilene, Texas 79699

1-877-816-4455 | www.leafwoodpublishers.com

19 20 21 22 23 24 / 7 6 5 4 3 2 1

CONTENTS

For John Brown—
A cherished mentor
A caring friend
A Christ-like brother

ACKNOWLEDGMENTS

In addition to thanking and praising God above all for bringing this work to fruition, I want to express my gratitude to a number of people.

Writing a book on the rhythm of the Christian life in eight weeks would not have been possible without a rhythm or (more importantly) *the* rhythm. Therefore, I'm grateful to my wife, Daniella, for helping me find a writing rhythm in the nooks and crannies of our life together with our four amazing children, Neriah, Zephaniah, Jedidiah, and Hezekiah. As for *the* rhythm, were it not for the back-and-forth harmony between my time alone with God and time together with others, this volume would not have been possible.

In order of how this project came together, I want to first express thanks to Jason Fikes. He sensed the potential for a book such as this before I ever wrote a sentence. Through numerous email correspondences and a delightful dinner in Colorado, we finalized the details and I began writing. Since then, Jason, Rebecka Scott, and the entire team at Leafwood have been a joy to work with, and I'm deeply appreciative of all their labors along the way.

I also want to thank Ken Bell, Christian Garabedian, Earon James, Randy Johnson, Joe Liechty, Frank Judice, Dennis Louis, Hannah Madeira, Grant Mayfield, Nathan Wagnon, and Joshua Wallnofer. They each sacrificed their time in order to discuss this project with me, exchange emails, and offer up intercessory prayers. All of those interactions and prayers helped me gain the focus and clarity that I would not have had alone. They also allowed me to experience firsthand what I was writing about in this book.

In addition, I am especially grateful to James Bradley for reading the first draft of each chapter. As embarrassing as that was for me, I'm sure glad I sent them to him. He provided me with some critical feedback early on, and graciously did so within such a short time frame.

I also want to express my deep gratitude to Thomas Williams and Michael Herrington. Tom's excellent developmental editing contributed significantly to the book being better than it would have been otherwise. Michael's keen eye for detail was key at the final stage of this work. His insights were all helpful and have been incorporated whenever possible.

Finally, I want to thank John Brown, to whom this book is dedicated. Beyond his encouragement and valuable input over those eight weeks of writing, his life over the past sixteen years that I've known him has modeled for me what the rhythm of the Christian life ought to look like. Indeed, he embodies those powerful words of Paul, "I always take pains to have a clear conscience toward both God and man" (Acts 24:16).

Soli Deo Gloria

FOREWORD

I first heard about Dietrich Bonhoeffer when I was a young college student seeking to know what it meant to follow Jesus in a world coming apart at the seams. I still have my red paperback edition of *The Cost of Discipleship*, which the cover described as "a powerful attack on 'easy Christianity' by a brilliant teacher and thinker." It proved to be all of that and more as I devoured what had already become a classic of Christian devotion and spiritual reading. First published in Munich in 1937, *Nachfolge*—the original one-word title in German—means literally "to follow after." Bonhoeffer was a theologian whose ideas were tested in a time of trouble. He spoke across the decades to my generation and still speaks today.

Later, when I was given the responsibility to develop a new theological school, another book by Bonhoeffer, *Life Together*, was chosen as the informal guide and manual for our fledgling enterprise. *Life Together* sums up how Bonhoeffer and the students gathered around him in the underground seminary in Nazi Germany organized their common life of prayer, study, worship, communion, and witness. This book begins with a verse from the Psalms: "Behold, how good and how pleasant it is for brethren to dwell together in unity!" (Ps. 133:1). One of the most important sections of the book bears the heading "Not an Ideal but a Divine Reality." Bonhoeffer's community was not perfect, and neither is ours. But we both recognize our common life in Jesus Christ as an incredible gift from God. As Bonhoeffer puts it, long before we entered into common life with one another, "God has bound us together in one body with other Christians in Jesus Christ."

In both of these seminal books, Bonhoeffer is saying that no one can be a Christian alone. As the ancient monks used to say, no one can wash his own feet. No one is an island—isolated, detached, sufficient unto itself. The body of Christ is just that, a body, a living organism with many parts, many millions of cells, tempered by the Creator to work together collaboratively and in harmony.

As there is a pattern of Christian truth revealed in God's written Word, the Bible, so too there is a pattern of Christian life, of life together. But Christian community should not be a well-organized and carefully managed association of people gathered to perform a function or achieve a stated goal. No, the Christian community is *koinonia*, a common sharing and participation in the Holy Spirit, the life of God himself. Within this life, there is a kind of rhythm, what Brian Wright describes in this book as being "in sync" with the pulsating life of the Spirit.

Solitude and fellowship, silence and speech, the active life of witness and mission together with the interior life of contemplation and reflection. One of these dimensions without the other does not lead to faithful discipleship.

What Wright offers is an incarnational model of following Jesus. This book assumes that Christianity is neither a philosophy of religion nor a code of behavior, but rather a relationship with the Triune God to which we are called, not as isolated individuals but as a company of faithful disciples, followers of Jesus Christ. In a world of distraction and minor absolutes, such a community is a signpost of hope and faithfulness.

—Timothy George

Founding Dean of the Beeson Divinity School of Samford University, Senior Theological Advisor for *Christianity Today*, and general editor of the *Reformation Commentary on Scripture*

RHYTHMS

Whoever thus serves Christ is acceptable to God and approved by men. —Romans 14:18

Who can really be faithful in great things if he has not learned to be faithful in the things of daily life?
—Dietrich Bonhoeffer, *Life Together*

A good life requires a good rhythm—a pattern of movement regularly repeated over time. When we live life in tempo and experience the various harmonies around us, we find true joy and experience lasting contentment. It is why we listen to music when we exercise and work—to give us a backbeat to our activities. It is why we keep calendars—to live in harmony with the seasons. It is why we schedule things—to get into a groove at home and work. It is why newborns are so exhausting—they disrupt all our rhythms. But when they (finally!) get on a feeding and sleeping schedule, the dark circles under our eyes vanish and life seems to be restored.

Rhythms exist in all areas of life. From simple lullabies to symphony orchestras, rhythmic music attracts us. It elevates our spirit and brings us closer to others. Even babies bounce in beat.

When we exercise for fitness, recreation, or competition, we are at our best when we hit our stride and harmonize our movements. We quickly learn about the relationship between breathing and technique. Success requires a good sequence between the two. If we do not take the appropriate amount of breaths at the proper time, we tire quickly. Tired arms and legs equal bad technique. Improper technique creates strain and failure. The relationship works both ways. If we begin with poor technique, it can create issues with breathing, which in turn makes us unproductive. In the end, we all need the harmonious flow between the two in order to thrive.

We also delight in watching others perfect various rhythms, accomplishing peak performance, like in the Olympic Games. Why is this so? What is it about someone else's balance, proportion, and symmetry that draws us in? We are drawn to their performance because we identify with, we feel—albeit at a distance—their cadence and ability to find the sweet spot. Whether in us or someone else, we take pleasure in such rhythms.

Thinking back on our lives, we can all recall certain sequences that had a positive influence on us. In everything that mattered, there was rhythm. For some, holiday seasons were the most rhythmical. If we take a moment to reflect, we can likely taste our favorite food, or smell the festive air around us. Our rich family traditions with loved ones have formed layers of memories that are still etched in our minds and remain priceless. Perhaps we now delight in seeing the wonder on the faces of our children and grandchildren as they experience these rhythms for the first time.

For others, the most memorable and valuable rhythms lie elsewhere. Perhaps it was finding the ideal daily routine for your children. Maybe it was the hopeful countdown of a New Year's Eve event, or the count to ten before "Ready or not, here I come!" Perhaps it was jumping rope with neighborhood friends. Maybe it was the beat of the drums as you played in a band or your boots hit the pavement as your unit marched in cadence, enabling you to perform better and last longer. Perhaps it was learning the steps of a dance with a loved one, teaching the ideal rhythm for CPR to save lives, or the consistency of receiving a regular paycheck.

Sadly, we often find ourselves out of sync and see others off beat. When our lives or bodies get imbalanced, life becomes unpleasant, unhealthy, and unsustainable. We suffer physically, mentally, emotionally, and spiritually. An irregular heartbeat can lead to a stroke or death. If we keep stepping on our partner's feet during a dance, then we will never find the beauty of synchronized movements. If we fail to find an athletic rhythm, then we will never achieve peak performance. When a toddler plays on a drum set, while perhaps their performance is funny and cute, they will not produce pleasing music. When someone insists on marching to his or her own beat, then he or she will get a life that is much harder and more problematic.

Suppose someone refuses software upgrades over time. His or her intentions might be good—disliking the thought of experiencing glitches, disrupting their established pattern of work, and spending the extra time on the time-consuming task of learning a new platform. But as a result, he or she is more vulnerable to security threats, misses a boost in program performance, and becomes disconnected with others. Life is harder when we chose to be out of sync with others.

Likewise, any imbalance of under- or overworking restricts our God-given potential. Throwing off our internal, biological clock (or circadian rhythms) can lead to weight gain, impulsive behavior, or other physiological and behavioral troubles. The list could go on.

The reason why the good life is rhythmic is because rhythm comes from God. Creation has predictable order because the Creator made it that way. God established the beats, pulses, surges, and sequences we all experience because he is a God of order, and every beautiful sequence points to him. Rhythm is engrained in our lives because God created us that way, and every good gift really does come from him.

As we witness the recurrent seasons, cyclical ocean tides, and planetary movements, we are seeing different patterns in nature that he formed. As we observe the day alternate with night, or track the monthly phases of the moon, we are in the midst of God's harmonious order. As we enjoy a natural sleep cycle or feel our hearts beating, lungs breathing, and eyes blinking regularly, we are experiencing several sequences of good health as he intended. As we try to imagine the continual cycles inside of our bodies that we cannot see or feel, such as metabolism, we are reminded that God cares about our daily life.

We see similarities in our spiritual lives. Scripture speaks of a weekly Sabbath day to rest from work and to intimately commune with God and his people. We read about the seasonal feasts, festivals, and fast God graciously instituted for his children to enjoy and connect better with him and others. There were cycles of extended rest that God commanded so the land could recover, poor people could gather food freely, animals could eat, and property would be restored (Lev. 25:1–17). We also see the daily hours of prayer—praying at regular intervals throughout the day—mentioned throughout Scripture.

Both naturally and spiritually, God intends for our lives to be lived in rhythm. Our bodies were built to work this way and our souls were fashioned to feel this way. Our Christian lives are meant to be lived in anticipation of and preparation toward the part of the cycle that is coming next. Knowing what to expect helps us feel safe, confident, and secure. Rhythm comes from God, and it is a gracious gift so that we can live fuller, richer, and healthier lives. True joy and a fully flourishing life only occur inside of God's ordained rhythms, for God wants us to be not only holy but whole.

The truth is that all of us find ourselves or see others out of balance at times. We stop living in—or worse, never find—the rhythm God intends for us. We start, or continue, living according to our own desires that are always out of balance and never in sync with God. We cannot glorify God—the chief purpose of our life—without living in the rhythm of faith he ordained. He wired us this way. He designed it into our DNA. As Christians, our whole life, no matter when or in what context, consists of loving God and loving others—just like Jesus did. When we neglect the rhythm of the Christian life as God ordained it, we are vulnerable to sin, Satan, and the world.

Thankfully, a saint who was especially sensitive to God's rhythms, and especially effective at helping others find God's groove, was Dietrich Bonhoeffer.

Bonhoeffer's Life

Dietrich Bonhoeffer was a pastor and scholar. He received advanced degrees, wrote a variety of books, and rubbed elbows with several of the greatest scholars of his day. At the same time, he prioritized local church ministry. He never forgot the people for whom Christ died. In 1930–31, instead of simply seeking academic honors and accolades during his short stay in America for some postgraduate studies, he got deeply involved in local church ministry. The church he served in was not one of the closer, more prestigious churches near Union Theological Seminary in New York where he studied. Rather, he went to a church in Harlem a couple of miles away. He went there because, unlike the other churches he visited, they preached the gospel and he saw it lived out among the people. He stayed actively involved by teaching a boys' Sunday school class there, as well as participating in a number of other church-related activities.

Upon his return to Germany in 1931, he continued serving in the church while advancing his academic career. He taught unruly children from one of the most impoverished parts of Berlin. Instead of simply showing up to teach them in their community and then returning to an affluent neighborhood afterward, he rented a place to stay where they lived. Instead of merely teaching them, he provided the boys pastoral care throughout the week, including multiple hospital visits when anyone was sick or had surgery. He taught them Christ in the classroom and showed them Christ in the community.

At one point in 1935, Bonhoeffer was given the unique opportunity to study under Mahatma Gandhi. He instead opted to direct an underground seminary initially at Zingst and then Finkenwalde, which became the backdrop to his *Life Together* book, with only a couple dozen students. As Hitler enhanced his army, some of Bonhoeffer's students were forced to join. Bonhoeffer wrote letters to them between 1936–42, encouraging them to minister faithfully no matter where they were placed. The Gestapo ordered the closure of the seminary in August 1937.

Bonhoeffer was not only kind but also brave in the extreme. After coming back to America in 1939 at the invitation of Union Theological Seminary, he said that he quickly regretted the decision. He determined that leaving Germany at such a difficult time under Nazi control was wrong. He could not imagine ministering there after the war if he had lived in comfort somewhere else while his brothers and sisters in Christ went through such tremendous sufferings. Bonhoeffer wrote in a letter to Reinhold Niebuhr, "I have made a mistake in coming to America. I must live through this difficult period in our national history with the Christian people of Germany. I will have no right to participate in the reconstruction of Christian life in Germany after the war if I do not share the trials of this time with my people."

Against the advice of his friends to stay in the United States and live the safe life of an academic, he returned to Germany that same year to continue his pastoral work. Little did he know that the decision not to choose the path of a scholar and stay in the ivory tower of isolated academic life would eventually cost him his life, as he was arrested by the Gestapo in 1943 and executed on April 9, 1945.

Bonhoeffer's *Life Together*

What Bonhoeffer lived out, he also described in his book *Life Together*. He genuinely captured the essence of Christian community and conveyed it in such a clear and compelling way that generations later it remains one of the best works on the character of Christian community. In just over a hundred pages, there are sections on the nature of Christian community, time spent in community with other believers, time spent alone with God, maintaining unity in ministry, even confession and communion.

But most relevant for our purposes are his sections on time together and time alone. Time together includes activities like communal reading, congregational singing, and collective praying. Time alone involves personal journaling, private reflection, and other individual disciplines.

Now, we may initially think that these two categories are nothing new. Today, we often describe the Christian life in similar ways: vertical and horizontal, heavenly and earthly, personal and interpersonal, individual and communal, private and public, quiet time and group time, secret worship and public worship. We may even find it odd that he has an entire chapter on being alone with God when his book is explicitly on Christian fellowship.

But therein lies a key aspect of his work: rather than dividing them into two separate categories, or only noting their general association, he connects the two together and stresses the pulsating flow between them. The rhythm of the Christian life is a biblically based, centuries-old belief that time alone with God and time together with others are intimately connected and work in tandem to glorify God.

When this sequence is separated into segments—even if just for the sake of explanation—we miss the beauty of the whole. Scripture never divides or confuses the two. Both the activities (things we do) and attitudes (our character qualities) surrounding our corporate and personal lives are linked in this foundational rhythm. The measured swing of a clock's pendulum illustrates clearly the necessary balance between our time together and time with God. This balance keeps the rhythm of the Christian life in sync and moves us toward a deeper and more meaningful spiritual life.

Although Bonhoeffer never uses the word "rhythm" in *Life Together*, he describes the pulsating flow of the Christian life as it swings back and forth from time together to time alone with God. They are as connected as inhaling and exhaling are to breathing, an inseparable relationship. He writes, for instance, "Only in the fellowship do we learn to be rightly alone and only in aloneness do we learn to live rightly in the fellowship. It is not as though the one preceded the other; both begin at the same time, namely, with the call of Jesus Christ." He began at the ground level, surveying for us the biblical text in relation to time alone and time together.

In his work, we learn that our private time with God is not *really* private. It is about more—far more—than just each one of us individually. "Time alone" is rightly understood only within the Christian community. It is a social, not just a personal, thing. In fact, the health of the community depends on each one of our private devotional lives. Everything we do (or don't do) affects both us individually and the church communally (for better or worse). What may seem at first glance a "personal" practice is actually communal in nature.

The same is true regarding our time together—it connects to and fosters our time alone. We cannot have one without the other, or we will be off-balance. To miss the importance and centrality of how these two principles work together is to misunderstand the distinctive nature of the rhythm of the Christian life. Or as Bonhoeffer puts it, "Blessed is he who is alone in the strength of the fellowship and blessed is he who keeps the fellowship in the strength of aloneness."

Despite the challenges and setbacks of his life, Bonhoeffer maintained gospel hope. His book remains a passionate plea from a pastor-scholar who truly believed and experienced the practical outworking of the rhythm of the Christian life. He taught it to pastors in training at both Zingst and Finkenwalde, enabling them to go and implement it in their congregations. The man was no fan of the kind of hands-off Christianity that lacks the robust relationships for which Christ died. He rebukes the idea that living within the Christian community is merely desirable—or even admirable—but not necessary. He calls us to realize what we really need, not what we *perceive* we need.

Embracing the rhythm of the Christian life, and living it wholeheartedly, is the task of all believers, not just some of us. It is not to be understood merely as a good idea in general, but it is to take on a specific shape in real circumstances.

It is also not just an ideal lived in the past when we had real heroes like Bonhoeffer. We still have such faithful believers today. In fact, already this year we saw the passing away of such a person: Thomas L. Phillips (1924–2019), the longtime chairman and CEO of Raytheon.

For all his accomplishments in the secular world, reaching what many would consider to be the pinnacle of business success, he considered his most significant achievements to be the things he did for the kingdom of God. For over forty years, he hosted a meeting once a month (deemed "First Tuesday") with young Christian leaders in the Boston area to help them develop their leadership skills according to the Christian faith. He served on the boards of many Christian organizations. He led Charles "Chuck" Colson to Christ after the Watergate scandal under President Richard Nixon.

Phillips lived a life worth living—one that alternated between time alone with God and time together with others. His life illustrates for us one of life's vital rhythms: the back-and-forth need for fellowship with God and fellowship with the Christian community.

SUMMARY

The rhythm of the Christian life expresses something that is universally important and true for every believer in Christ: the harmonious flow and strong connection between our time alone with God and time spent with one another. This divine tempo is timeless and transcends cultures. Although the pace of life might be different depending on where we live—perhaps a big city like New York, London, or Tokyo, where most people walk fast, overschedule, double-book, and multitask, or somewhere more secluded, like a small town in Alaska, a remote village in India, or a far-flung district in Peru—the underlying beat is the same and it is no less musical.

The rhythm of our life will lead to either blessing or disaster. Sin destroys our cadence and the cascading consequences of falling out of balance are catastrophic. But Christ redeems the rhythm, and by God's grace, we can still integrate it in our life as he intends. By holistically understanding the rhythm of the Christian life, we move from surface living into the depths of life—from splashing around in the shallows with our floaties on, to going out twenty thousand leagues under the sea.

Of course, we cannot approach God or be reconciled to each other except through Christ. We cannot know or examine ourselves properly except with Jesus's help. Without him, we cannot have time alone or time together as we should. In Christ alone, we are alone in Christ. In Christ alone, we are together in Christ. We only become one in the One and Only. We live, move, and exist in him (Col. 1:17). Jesus is the author of life (Acts 3:15); founder of our salvation (Heb. 2:10); perfecter of our faith (Heb. 12:2).

The rhythm of the Christian life is as vital to the health of each individual and the entire body of Christ, as a regular heartbeat is to the health of every part of one's body. Growth in faith does not come about *in vitro*. It occurs in the womb of the church and is the work of the whole community. In other words, we know that we cannot generate faith or cause growth by our own devices the way laboratories foster human conception in a test tube. Faith is always the work of God, planted in the womb of the church and nurtured in growth and maturity by the entire community.

The rhythm of the Christian life connects humanity's two fundamental relationships. We only become truly ourselves when we exist for God and others. Therefore, we must strengthen and enlarge the rhythmic relationship between them in our lives. We must grasp this pride-shattering and community-enhancing pattern and live it wholeheartedly. The result is a spiritual life that transforms our community, the world, and us.

TIME TOGETHER

Whoever loves God must also love his brother. —1 John 4:21

It is grace, nothing but grace, that we are allowed to live in community with Christian brethren.

—Dietrich Bonhoeffer, *Life Together*

Spending time with people is better than anything else in this world. The best entertainment, finest food, and greatest wealth all mean nothing in comparison to our family and friends. Most of us can attest to this. Our fondest memories recall times when we were with people. Our closest friends and loved ones brought us sheer joy. We can still hear the sound of their laughter. We can see the expressions on their face. We can taste the drinks and foods we shared with them.

We have had special people in our lives who helped us far more than any pleasures, health, or wealth. If we take a moment to reflect on the relationships God has graciously granted us, we can think of people who contributed to where we are today. Maybe a teacher offered words of encouragement. Perhaps a supervisor provided an opportunity to advance professionally. Maybe a dear friend stuck close when everyone else fled.

There can be little doubt that King David experienced this with Jonathan. They shared one of the deepest, most meaningful friendships described in the Bible. Right between the times of David being betrayed by the people in the town of Keilah and then by the Ziphites, Scripture highlights how David persevered: "Jonathan, Saul's son, rose and went to David at Horesh, and strengthened his hand in God" (1 Sam. 23:16).

Imagine if this was the last time you saw one of your closest friends. He or she came to your aide, strengthened you in the Lord, and you never saw them again. As far as Scripture reveals, it was for David. The next mention of Jonathan is the report of his death (31:2).

We all recall people who truly cared about us and wanted what was best for us in life. They inspired us to keep going, and encouraged us never to give up. It is a privilege to have others in our lives, and they are often a key source of our strength and happiness.

Beyond the laughter, closeness, and good times spent together are the memories of how those times influenced us. Someone pulled us aside and helped us see God's will more clearly. We got helpful advice on what we should do next in a situation that would alter the course of our lives. We learned more about ourselves as we listened to them. We received tips on how to do something, or recommendations on where else to turn when all hope seemed lost. The greatest memories we have of times with others are likely the ones with the most depth.

Do you remember me sharing in Chapter One that Raytheon CEO Tom Phillips led Chuck Colson to Christ? As Colson later described the full story, Phillips pulled him aside one night and spoke to him eyeball to eyeball. This was before Colson went off to serve his time in a maximum security state penitentiary. Phillips ultimately told Colson that he got into the mess he was in because he lost perspective, as if God was not over him and other people did not matter. Phillips shared that there was only one solution for Colson, just as there is for everyone else: believing in Jesus Christ.

After their discussion, Colson said he got into his car, put his head on the steering wheel, and wept until he could weep no more. There, he prayed his first real prayer, simply asking God to take his life and do with it as he wills. He never forgot the depth of that time together with Phillips, who pulled him aside and set him on a new course in life. He also never forgot how it flowed right into his first time alone with God—physically alone on a dark night without any sense of being alone.

The same phenomenon has probably happened to countless others, maybe even you. In those trying seasons of life when temptations seemed to overwhelm you, it only took that certain person to walk into the room to calm you down and bring peace to the situation. His or her comforting embrace, challenging words, or quiet presence did far more for you than anything else. Those difficult times were overcome because God's grace put specific people in your path. And, of course, God has graciously used you when you have served, encouraged, and helped others. God has masterfully designed you to be built up in community so that you can build up the community.

The point in all this is that we all are deeply indebted to certain people with whom we spent time. And with God's grace, we, too, can play a vital role in the lives of those around us, as well as those who come after us. Our life is grander than we ever imagined, extending both backward and forward in time. We play a vital role between the two. As we draw both inspiration and instruction from those who have gone before us, we consider the people who will one day be nourished and encouraged by the way we stewarded God's call on our life. We have been given gifts, talents, and a role to play among God's faithful that spans generations, not to lie dormant and be enjoyed for ourselves but to be shared communally with others so that our joy may be full.

Scripture and history both offer glorious examples of people doing the very thing we are just reminiscing about here: heeding God's call to spend purposeful time together with other believers—praying, serving, celebrating, confessing, studying, sharpening.

Imagine for a moment what might have become of Samuel had Eli not been there to guide him in discerning God's call on his life (1 Sam. 3). Suppose King David never spent time together with Nathan, who rebuked David's great wrongdoing with a shattering revelation (1 Sam. 12). Picture what could have happened to the Ethiopian eunuch had he remained alone in the chariot without his time together with Philip (Acts 8). Consider how different

Apollos's ministry would have been without his time together with Priscilla and Aquila (Acts 18). What would have ever happened to Augustine without fellow believers in his life like Ambrose; Luther without Melanchthon; Calvin without Farel; Bonhoeffer without Bethge? Praise God, we will never know!

What was true at the individual level was also true at the community level. After long months of living in small groups, all the people of Israel would heed God's command to meet together three times a year as a larger— confessionally united—body (Exod. 23:14). Right after establishing the importance of a long list of individuals in chapter 2 (vv. 1–70), Ezra makes it a point to emphasize their corporate unity and common faith by saying in the first verse of the next chapter, "the people gathered *as one man* to Jerusalem" (Ezra 3:1; italics added).

Imagine what these great annual gatherings would have been like for the people of God. The Feast of Tabernacles, for instance, was a joyous time when God's people got out of their houses and lived for a week in makeshift tents—reminding them in part where they came from and all that God had done for them. It marked the end of harvest time, and was a festival of rejoicing in response to God's blessings (Deut. 16:15).

Picture the camaraderie, the tales around the campfires, the hand-held snack foods, perhaps playing games throughout the days with music and dancing well into the torch-lit evenings. So popular was this holiday that God's people from remote villages like Galilee would make the seventy-mile (or more) trip up to Jerusalem to celebrate it even during war times. In fact, we know that Jesus made the trek from Galilee to Jerusalem for this feast (John 7).

Those outside the covenant community noticed their communal life together as well. The wicked prophet Balaam observed this about Israel: "Here is a people living alone, and not reckoning itself among the nations!" (Num. 23:9). There was a separated character about them communally in a positive sense. In their set-apartness, they were not like everyone else in the world as they did life together. They did more than exist in close geographical proximity. They also shared the joys of life together with one another—beckoning each other to God.

As we will see, it has always been God's intention that his children spend intentional time with both believers and nonbelievers. Based on the principle of the rhythm of the Christian life, it is clear that God intends our time spent in community with others to foster and benefit our time spent alone with him. Just as an engine charges a battery and a battery sparks an engine, the reciprocal influence of this rhythm is necessary to keep our spiritual life running. This reciprocal influence is powerful.

But before we discuss what our time together with others is supposed to look like and how it complements our time alone with God in the overall rhythm of the Christian life (Chapter Four), let us remove the false ideas that might otherwise hinder our progress and consider some examples from Scripture of spending time together with others.

Relinquishing Our Unrealistic Expectations

We all come to the Christian community with a host of expectations. We expect people to be welcoming, but we leave feeling excluded. We imagine that plugging in somewhere will be easy, but it is complicated. We think that conversations will flow naturally, but they are awkward. We assume relationships will go deeper and deeper, yet they remain shallow. We anticipate positive responses to our invitations for people to get together, only to find that no one responds or is interested in coming. We presume the whole community is healthy, but it isn't. And so forth.

The Christian community disappoints all of us at times. We all have examples of experiences that have left us disappointed, perhaps even causing us to shy away from full participation.

Granted, maybe there was something fundamentally wrong with a church we attended, such as heresy or immorality. But more often than not, the real problem was probably our own unrealistic expectations. That is why it is helpful for us to recognize that there is often a profound difference between the reality of the Christian community and our idea of it. In fact, Bonhoeffer would ask us to stop living in a dream world of what we think Christian community is, and instead, embrace the imperfect, messy, broken, and mistake-prone bride of Christ (the church). He writes:

> Every human wish dream that is injected into
> the Christian community is a hindrance to
> genuine community and must be banished
> if genuine community is to survive. He who
> loves his dream of a community more than
> the Christian community itself becomes a
> destroyer of the latter, even though his personal

intentions may be ever so honest and earnest and sacrificial.

Instead of pulling up our anchor and going elsewhere anytime we are let down by our community or feel a breeze we might not like, we must accept the periodic disappointments. Rather than cruising around looking for the "ideal" church, we must embrace the reality of the real Christian community.

This applies to newcomers, seekers, and new Christians, as well as regular churchgoers. The brand-new Christian, for instance, may come to the church with a host of preconceptions—lacking the maturity to have the kind of realism about the church that we are describing here. One church body might have arthritis; the next one measles; another one bronchitis. The more seasoned Christian, on the other hand, is rightly urged to exercise realism and maturity—taking in stride the human weaknesses that exist in every church. We are still brothers and sisters in Christ. No church is perfect, and Jesus deserves more than our bare minimum.

The goal is not finding a church that meets all of our expectations, scratches all of our itches, or accommodates all of our likes. The purpose of our gathering is to honor and glorify God in accordance with his written Word. We may not like the preaching or music selection, but what a great time for us to learn humility. We may not enjoy this or that person, but what a wonderful opportunity for us to become more like Christ in our love for others. We also cannot forget that to someone else, we are the person he or she struggles to love.

Spending time with people presents its challenges. We may at times leave our community stewing in anger at how things were done or what people were doing that we felt were wrong or misguided. But life is still best lived with others, and God commands us to do so. Fellowship with God means fellowship with his children. The Apostle John put it this way, "If we walk in the light, as he is in the light, we have fellowship with one another" (1 John 1:7). We cannot have it any other way.

At the same time, attending or becoming a member of a church does not mean we will immediately, or even permanently, feel connected. We might feel like a Lego piece that can fit anywhere, and perhaps we get the impression that we can just occasionally assemble and connect together with others in order to do something specific or look a certain way. The truth is, we are more like a puzzle piece that can fit only in one specific place in one specific puzzle. We cannot attach to another puzzle (for there is only One), and we each have a specific place we fit. Bonhoeffer puts it like this:

> In a Christian community everything depends upon whether each individual is an indispensable link in a chain. Only when even the smallest link is securely interlocked is the chain unbreakable.

Removing our unrealistic expectations will allow us to see the blessings of living together, the consequences of when we do not, and free us to return when we mess up.

Time Together with Believers

God created us in his image to live in community, and he wants his children to spend time together in unity. When he calls us to himself, we are directed to each other. We are to be "with" and "for" one another. When we are, it is a wonderful thing—fulfilling our longing for belonging. We experience more of God's precious gifts, and our lives are more joyous, rich, healthy, and meaningful. God uses others to bless us, and he uses us to bless others—the flow is reciprocal.

Wonderfully in Sync

So what does the Bible say about time together as God's children? As we open up God's Word, we see his will expressed throughout Scripture. Let me highlight a few stories for you from both the Old Testament and New Testament.

Old Testament

In the beginning, God, Adam, and Eve were in perfect harmony. Later, we see Moses and Aaron, both in their eighties, working in tandem to fulfill God's will in delivering his people (Exod. 6:30–7:7). Moses's final blessing on Israel begins with the reminder that "the LORD became king in Jeshurun, when the heads of the people were gathered, all the tribes of Israel together" (Deut. 33:5).

We continue to see that as God's people obey him and live in community with one another, they reap his blessings. In 2 Chronicles, it is noteworthy that when Rehoboam and the princes of Israel humbled themselves *together*, they were delivered (2 Chron. 12). When Asa and all of Judah turned from their wicked ways *together*, the Lord gave them rest all around (2 Chron. 15). When Jehoshaphat and all of Judah and Jerusalem sought God's face *in unity*, they beheld the salvation of the Lord (2 Chron. 20). When Hezekiah prays *together* with Isaiah, the Lord saves the people of Jerusalem and exalts Hezekiah before all the nations (2 Chron. 32).

After Israel's exile, Nehemiah coordinated the rebuilding of the walls in Jerusalem, and when the prophet Ezra read the Law, everyone came together "as one man" (emphasizing their collective unity) and their weeping turned into great rejoicing (Neh. 8).

In the book of Job, it is significant to observe that Job's friend, Eliphaz the Temanite, mentions how many people were blessed when they spent time together with Job. He instructed many people, strengthened their weak hands, upheld those who were stumbling, and made feeble knees steady again (Job 4:3–4).

In the book of Psalms, King David's waiting on God is not done privately but communally: "I am like a green olive tree in the house of God. . . . I will wait for your name, for it is good, in the presence of the godly" (Ps. 52:8–9). He takes his private vows into the sanctuary among faithful believers—in the house of God with God's people. He knew that a flourishing life is one that lives in the company of God while living in the presence of God's people. He sought to surround himself with people who shared the same spiritual convictions—both those who dwelt with him and worked for him (101:6). He expressed his delight when he was invited by others to go to the house of the Lord:

> I was glad when they said to me,
>> "Let us go to the house of the LORD!"
> Our feet have been standing
>> within your gates, O Jerusalem!
> Jerusalem—built as a city
>> that is bound firmly together,
> to which the tribes go up,
>> the tribes of the LORD,
> as was decreed for Israel,
>> to give thanks to the name of the LORD.
>> (Ps. 122:1–4)

There was a depth of joy from worshipping together that David could not get by himself, and he concludes the song with a focus on what he does for the sake of others (vv. 8–9). Later in the Psalms, David also describes for us how dwelling together in unity is good, pleasant, luxurious, and refreshing (Ps. 133).

In the book of Isaiah, as God's people see the return of the Lord to Zion together "eye to eye," there is singing, joy, comfort, and redemption (Isa. 52:8). In Micah and Zephaniah, God expresses his desire for his people to assemble together and details the blessings that will follow:

> I will surely assemble all of you, O Jacob;
>> I will gather the remnant of Israel;
> I will set them together
>> like sheep in a fold,

> like a flock in its pasture,
>> a noisy multitude of men. (Mic. 2:12)

> At that time I will bring you in,
>> at the time when I gather you together;
> for I will make you renowned and praised
>> among all the peoples of the earth,
> when I restore your fortunes
>> before your eyes. (Zeph. 3:20)

God wants to gather us, not condemn us. He offers security—not destruction—through trusting in him. Like a mother bird, to use familiar biblical imagery, God seeks to unify and protect us (Deut. 32:11; Isa. 31:5).

The Old Testament ends with the book of Malachi, and the prophet writes this about God's people coming together:

> Then those who feared the LORD spoke with one another. The LORD paid attention and heard them, and a book of remembrance was written before him of those who feared the LORD and esteemed his name. (3:16)

Unlike the larger group of people who opposed God and his commands, here is a remnant of believers who "spoke with one another" in community. This was no everyday chitchat. It was a communal reasoning together among believers united in faith, signifying a harmonious reciprocity.

New Testament

The New Testament emphasizes the same divine desire for God's redeemed children to spend time together, and the amazing blessings that flow in, through, and to them. Jesus modeled and taught it best, as seen in the four Gospels. He invested in others, especially the twelve disciples, and even more in the three closest to him (Peter, John, and James). He spent time with them. He prayed for them. He empowered them. He taught them. He showed them how to live. All of them were blessed together as they learned the truth, were served sacrificially, and received empowerment for ministry. He expected them to go and do likewise with others.

When the early church was in a habit of spending time together, and not just weekly or biweekly, "the Lord added to their number day by day those who were being saved" (Acts 2:46–47). At the same time, the fellowship of the saints was not measured by numbers but by intensity. They shared worship, meals, prayer, and possessions together. They traveled together. God responded to their prayers to release Peter from prison (Acts 12:11). Later, when Paul and Silas prayed together, they also were released from prison (Acts 16:24–34).

Even activities such as reading were often more fruitful when done communally than individually. Reading together aided understanding of Scripture, as it did when Philip and the Ethiopian official studied the scroll of Isaiah while traveling down the road in a chariot (Acts 8:31; cf. Luke 24:32). It fostered social networking and community connections, as it did when Paul tells the Christians in Colossae to exchange his letters with the church in Laodicea after reading them (Col. 4:16). It allowed believers to discuss their common confession, as it did for the recipients of the letter to the Hebrews (Heb. 3:1). By reading in community, believers were able to:

- settle debates (Acts 15:16–30)
- rejoice together (Acts 15:31)
- maintain unity in diversity (Acts 15:33)
- bring the light of Christ to an unbelieving world (Acts 17:2)
- commend people (Rom. 16:1–2)
- understand Paul's insights into the mystery of Christ (Eph. 3:4)

All the apostles cherished spending time together with others in Christian community. Reflecting on his time in Corinth, Paul expresses the joy he and Timothy shared in being connected to fellow believers there: "I said before that you are in our hearts, to die together and to live together" (2 Cor. 7:3). Paul informs us that as we are "nourished and knit together," we grow "with a growth that is from God" (Col. 2:19). He reminds us that we remain connected to the greater, universal body of Christ even at times when we cannot be present with members of our own congregation or even other churches. And our prayers and passion for all our fellow believers should continue (Rom. 15:22–24; Col. 2:5).

John tells us he has "no greater joy" than to hear testimonies of others and how they are walking in the truth (3 John 3–4). Being one together in Christ is not some idea to be pondered but a present reality in which we must participate. There are no vestigial organs in the body of Christ. Even people separated from other believers outside their control (like missionaries in prison) are functioning members of the one flock of God (1 Cor. 12:20). When Paul was physically absent from Colossae while on house arrest, he still had an overwhelming sense of connectedness. He writes, "For though I am absent in body, yet I am with you in spirit" (Col. 2:5).

Luke highlights the fact that we are empowered by the Spirit when we are together (Acts 8:14–17; 10:44–47; 15:8). If someone is ill and unable to be together with other believers, there is "sorrow upon sorrow" (Phil. 2:27; see also 1 Cor. 12:26). One reason why we faithfully pass on sound biblical teaching is so that our brothers and sisters in Christ will not depart from the fellowship and follow the lies and lures of this world's false teachers (1 Tim. 4:6).

Even the physical touch of a believer can be a great blessing. Beyond the ministry of Jesus, and the "mighty works done by his hands" (Mark 6:2; cf. Luke 6:19; 8:46), blessings via physical touch were frequent. When the apostles prayed for those appointed as deacons, they placed their hands upon them (Acts 6:6). By God's grace, Paul and Barnabas performed many signs and wonders "by their hands" (Acts 14:3). Timothy received a spiritual gift when elders laid their hands on him (1 Tim. 4:14).

Meaningful touch fosters connection even today. It includes not only the laying on of hands but also handshakes, hugs, pats on the back, a hand on a shoulder, and maybe even high-fives. All are expressions of love and caring, which foster community.

A major cure for many of our troubles is deep fellowship with God's people, our brothers and sisters in Christ. Perhaps we are weighed down with doubts; our hearts have become hardened; we are financially strapped.

Whatever the ills in our lives may be, strong Christian fellowship lightens the load, and sometimes it even cures the ill altogether. There is joy when we see others (2 Tim. 1:4; 2 John 12), cheerfulness when we hear good news about them (Phil. 2:19), and encouragement when we know others are genuinely concerned for our welfare (Phil. 2:20).

Believers express their faith with an unqualified hospitality, such as when a woman named Lydia invited some brothers in Christ to come and stay at her house right after she believed and was baptized (Acts 16:14–15). The author of 3 John commends Gaius for such unique hospitality, serving other brothers and sisters in Christ "even though they are strangers" (3 John 5). The common core of Christian community is Christ, and that frees us to love and serve one another. When we see others alone, like widows and orphans, we are not content in leaving them in that condition (James 1:27).

Betsie ten Boom and her sister Corrie lived this out well while they were imprisoned together under Nazi forces. The sisters lived under some of the most miserable and depressing conditions—cramped quarters infested with fleas, among other things. Yet they still found comfort and joy in the Christian fellowship they had in prison—studying Scripture and singing praises with other believing prisoners. Their mutual bond in Christ was a means of their perseverance, especially as it was connected to and swung back-and-forth in tandem with their time alone with God.

From the moment of our conversion, each of us exists as an intimately connected part of a community of believers because "he who is joined to the Lord becomes one spirit with him" (1 Cor. 6:17). As soon as we enter that community, God blesses us. We are part of all the "one another" statements in the New Testament because we are with one another. We love one another. We honor one another. We serve one another. We build up one another. We encourage one another. We pray for one another. We give to one another.

On top of these blessings, James tells us that healing and forgiveness can be found when we are in Christian community (James 5:14–15). John lets us know that as we spend time together, loving one another, we can have assurance of our salvation (1 John 4:12–21).

In order to see ourselves correctly, we need community. When we see ourselves correctly in relation to others, more of God's precious gifts are revealed. As we receive these gifts, they are multiplied in our lives and the lives of those around us. We are formed in and by community. God does not just give us his Word to carry us through our trials. He also gives us each other. This is why godly men and women would not want to live without God's people; it would disrupt the divine rhythm of the Christian life.

To be sure, certain details of our life are not for everyone—our addictions, infidelities, doubts, experiences of abuse, criminal history, broken relationships, marriage or parenting struggles. Yet we all should have, just as Jesus did, an inner circle of trusted friends within our close-knit community. We can openly share our personal matters with those few fellow believers with whom we are especially close because we know nothing shared will go beyond them and they will strengthen us in God.

Among other things, our time together, whether in a church that is small or large, brings healing and meets needs. Simply put, life is great when we dwell together in unity! But what if we do not dwell together? What if we miss the remarkable experiences that occur in community?

Painfully out of Sync

As seen, there is nothing as heartwarming or soul satisfying as fellowship. But oftentimes, we just walk by it without stopping to be warmed by it. Then our souls are left cold and discontent. Worse, sometimes we fall away from the fellowship—dismissing God's people from the picture entirely. Perhaps we become wise in our own eyes, assuming we do not need help, counsel, or correction from anyone else (Prov. 26:12; Isa. 5:21). When that happens, life is not good and relationships are bad between God and others. Loneliness makes life worse, because it interrupts God's intended rhythm for us.

Picture a family whose life is a constant flurry of activity—working, taking care of children, doing housework, running errands, buying groceries. Something has to give, so it's fellowship. They don't attend church events because they "can't find time." Soon, the lack of connection makes it easy to miss classes, and then church assemblies. As their church relationships grow distant, their spiritual life begins to wither. They lose their original enthusiasm for connection, for Christ, and their spiritual flame finally burns low, flickers, and goes out.

Yes, fellowship is difficult for families like that, but it must be a priority over some of their other activities

("Martha, Martha . . ."; Luke 10:41). The Bible says the one who separates himself or herself from time together is a fool: "Whoever isolates himself seeks his own desire; he breaks out against all sound judgment" (Prov. 18:1). Warnings such as these in Scripture abound. Consider the words of the Preacher: "Woe to him who is alone when he falls and has not another to lift him up!" (Eccl. 4:10).

The Bible is equally as clear that the type of company we maintain is of utmost importance. It is not enough just to be around people—we must be around certain people. The book of Proverbs puts it this way: "the companion of fools will suffer harm" (Prov. 13:20). Paul shares these words: "Bad company ruins good morals" (1 Cor. 15:33). These principles apply to group gatherings and individual friendships.

The Bible is clear that God can hate our gatherings, reject our offerings, and refuse to listen to our songs (Amos 5:21–23). It is possible to be gathered together in disobedience against God or others (Num. 14:35; 16:3, 11; 21:23). The Psalmist on one occasion puts it like this: "They have all fallen away; together they have become corrupt" (Ps. 53:3). God may even say again as he did in the book of Isaiah: "Take counsel together, but it will come to nothing" (Isa. 8:10).

Just because a community or church unites in something does not mean it is a good thing (Judg. 9:6) or is from God (1 Sam. 8:4). Without God's help and guidance, we may deceive ourselves into thinking God is on our side when he is not, as Saul did (1 Sam. 23:7). We may accept the false claims of people who try to convince us that God is speaking to them when he is not, like the self-proclaimed false prophet who extends hospitality (1 Kings 13:18). We can also spend time with close friends who have good motives, but their advice and counsel end up being horrible and harmful (Job 2:11).

The goal, then, is not just to congregate with people or be social with someone. In today's church, this may even include such familiar church activities as teen pizza parties, group game nights, or church sporting events. It could be just about any get-together that seems to indicate spiritual content or connection but lacks it, like perhaps study groups led by unqualified leaders.

The key point here is not *that* we gather but *why* we gather. Some gatherings may do more harm than good. Recall the church in Corinth. The problem was not a failure to convene as a church but a failure to live as God's children when they were meeting (1 Cor. 11:17). In other words, they succeeded in coming together but failed to live as God's redeemed people when they gathered. Or perhaps a group of outwardly religious people come together, like false prophets, but they never embrace time together through faith. They maintain company and spend time together, but they forever fail because their band of intimate friends is not of the community of faith united in a relationship with God (Ezek. 13:9).

The dangers in all this are evident. We keep looking for the ideal instead of living in the reality. We accept the false idea that just because we go to a physical location for church that means we are involved in Christian community. That would be like going to a movie theater or sports stadium and thinking that our watching the movie or game equals being in the movie or playing on the field.

We wrongly think that just being involved in church activities equals a positive Christian communal experience. We sinfully get into comparison and triumphalism (even then, often to a false image of our community). We begin living in constant (electronic) community, or connect more digitally than deeply. We seek community simply as an antidote to our loneliness rather than for spiritual connection. We over-diversify our relationships so that we get to "know" everyone, building a never-ending stream of shallow relationships.

It is also possible that we create a demonic form of community. We become sectarian under the guise of being holy. We have an "us four and no more" mentality, losing our sense of missions and evangelism. We attend events together, and we are only there for each other with food and promises of prayer if there is an emergency. But we rarely go beyond that.

Seldom do we inconvenience ourselves with daily accountability, as we are commanded (Heb. 3:13). Rarely do we confront a brother or sister with a sinful practice in their lives, as we are instructed (Matt. 18:15). Hardly ever do we confess our sins to one another in a transparent way, though we should (James 5:16).

How many professing Christians confess their love for one another and their neighbor, but remain divided or distant in actual practice? How many times are divisive conversations held about others with whom we share communion? How often, in the process of multiplying our people and small groups, do we lose much depth—of relationships, doctrine, discipleship, generosity, prayer? Width without depth is deceptive (Matt. 13:1–9).

Note as well, we are commanded to avoid spending time with certain people. Contrary to popular culture, the Psalmist even equates godliness with the ability to spiritually discern the difference between vile people and honorable people (Ps. 15:4). In the New Testament, some of the strongest language in this regard was from Paul, Silvanus, and Timothy to the Thessalonian church. They don't just softly appeal to the church as in matters elsewhere, but strongly assert, "Now we command you, brothers, in the name of our Lord Jesus Christ, that you keep away from any brother who is walking in idleness and not in accord with the tradition that you received from us" (2 Thess. 3:6). Again, in verse 14, they say, "If anyone does not obey what we say in this letter, take note of that person, and have nothing to do with him, that he may be ashamed" (2 Thess. 3:14).

The idea of avoiding certain people occurs in almost every book in the New Testament, and we ought not to put a question mark where God puts a period. For instance, Paul's final instructions to the believers in Rome includes this: "I appeal to you, brothers, to watch out for those who cause divisions and create obstacles contrary to the doctrine that you have been taught; avoid them" (Rom. 16:17). He writes to the church in Corinth, "I am writing to you not to associate with anyone who bears the name brother if he is guilty of sexual immorality or greed, or is an idolater, reviler, drunkard, or swindler—not even to eat with such a one" (1 Cor. 5:11). After discussing people who love pleasure rather than God, he writes to Timothy, "Avoid such people" (2 Tim. 3:5). He writes to Titus, "As for a person who stirs up division, after warning him once and then twice, have nothing more to do with him" (Titus 3:10). The author of 2 John writes, "If anyone comes to you and does not bring this teaching, do not receive him into your house or give him any greeting" (v. 10).

On the contrary, we reach wise resolutions when we spend time together with those seeking God's counsel (Prov. 15:22); for they know that only God's plans will ultimately succeed (Prov. 19:21; cf. Acts 15:6, 31). Indeed, even angels spend time together in counsel with the Lord who is ultimately in charge (Ps. 89:7). But beyond mere statements about it, we see this need for the strength and wisdom gained from community played out in life. From Genesis to Revelation, we see numerous men and women forsake or fall away from the fellowship, and it always ends up disastrous if there is not a return to the community. Indeed, they are thrown out of whack and never adapt to the rhythm again.

We learn this fact from the life of Uzziah. He prospered when he was in community, but failed when he went off on his own. For the greater part of his reign (some forty years), he was seeking the Lord "in the days of Zechariah, who instructed him in the fear of God" (2 Chron. 26:5). Uzziah's spiritual welfare was so closely linked with Zechariah's godly influence that Scripture highlights it, like King Joash and Jehoiada the priest (2 Chron. 24:2). When Uzziah was in close fellowship with this godly person Zechariah, he won battles, rebuilt towns and towers, gained a great reputation, had plenty of livestock, employed many people, and led an impressive army. Because of that verse, we can presume that had their friendship not ended, Uzziah's life would not have ended as a tragic downfall. Had he only replaced Zechariah instead of isolating himself from such godly influences, Uzziah's life might have turned out differently.

Alas, while in his mid-fifties, Uzziah grew proud of his power and authority. His primary focus was on himself. He was preoccupied with getting his way. He disregarded the boundaries God established when he "entered the temple of the LORD to burn incense on the altar of incense" (26:16). He rejected the godly rebuke of eighty-one priests who were men of valor, and got angry with them. His individual "strength" and communal weakness was his downfall. He could not say no to himself, even when others tried to intervene. As a result, Uzziah spent the last ten years of his life under the judgment of God as a leper, living in a separate house, and excluded from the house of the Lord. He had lost the time together aspect of the rhythm.

If we keep reading in 2 Chronicles, Uzziah's grandson Ahaz did not dwell in the community of the faithful, but instead walked in the ways of the kings of Israel, and judgment fell on him (2 Chron. 28). Zedekiah refused to humble himself before other believers such as Jeremiah the prophet, and judgment fell on him (2 Chron. 36). Staying separated from God's people has never worked out well for long.

The same problem occurred after the exile. As we saw in Chapter One, God instituted a weekly Sabbath day to rest from work and to intimately commune with God and his people. Forsaking God's command to observe the Sabbath as a gathered community contravenes his plan to restore the world from the effects of sin.

In the book of Nehemiah, we read that one of the causes for God's judgment is not keeping the Sabbath day holy. Beyond the display of doubt, among other things, it breaks the rhythm God lays out for his people made in his image. Nehemiah writes this at the conclusion of his work:

> Then I confronted the nobles of Judah and said to them, "What is this evil thing that you are doing, profaning the Sabbath day? Did not your fathers act in this way, and did not our God bring all this disaster on us and on this city? Now you are bringing more wrath on Israel by profaning the Sabbath." (13:17–18)

God's people are called to trust him in the midst of this world. We must recognize that he is Lord of our time, and he calls us to spend time alone with him and time together with others whether we feel like it or not.

In the early church, a husband and wife named Ananias and Sapphira conspired apart from the accountability of the community (Acts 5). Instead of loving and engaging the Christian community like Barnabas, who sold some of his property and gave it to the apostles to distribute to those in need (Acts 4:37), they were distant and greedy—holding back for themselves some of the proceeds from their sale, assuming no one in the community would know. They both died that day.

People in Asia, like Phygelus and Hermogenes (probably known coworkers or church leaders), withdrew from Paul and his teaching, and thus from Christ (2 Tim. 1:15). A man named Demas was in solid fellowship with other believers, like Paul, Mark, and Luke (Philem. 24 and Col.

4:14). Then his love for the world became his downfall. He chose earthly comforts over heavenly rewards (2 Tim. 4:10), and we do not know what became of him. The words of the Psalmist ring true here:

> The righteous shall see and fear,
>   and shall laugh at him, saying,
> "See the man who would not make
>   God his refuge,
> but trusted in the abundance of his riches
>   and sought refuge in his own destruction!"
>   (Ps. 52:6–7)

Although God knows who his children are (2 Tim. 2:19), we Christians cannot always be so sure. Some who may appear to be authentic Christians are merely counterfeits. The author of 1 John says, "They went out from us, but they were not of us; for if they had been of us, they would have continued with us. But they went out, that it might become plain that they all are not of us" (1 John 2:19). Their willful, unrepentant disassociation from the church is evidence that they are not genuine believers.

But what if you find yourself in a period of disassociation with the body of Christ? What if your own fellowship with others seems frayed, distant, tenuous, or even severed?

Hopefully Re-synced

Rarely does God permit or instruct someone to stay in seclusion, as he did John the Baptist. When Hagar fled because Sarai was treating her poorly (Gen. 16:6), the angel of the Lord told her to "return" (Gen. 16:9). After

Moses fled to Midian because he feared Pharaoh (Exod. 2:15), the Lord ultimately told him to "go back" (Exod. 4:19). Elijah ran away because he was afraid of Jezebel (1 Kings 19:3), and after asking him twice, "What are you doing here, Elijah?" the Lord commanded him, "Go, return" (1 Kings 19:15).

We must not think all hope is lost when we recognize we have fallen away from the fellowship. We must stop doing as we please and return to the all-important rhythm of the Christian life. Instead of retreating into a private corner, we must reunite with the community—for a Christian without community is like a song without melody. Hear afresh the words God spoke through the prophet Isaiah:

> If you turn back your foot from the Sabbath,
>   from doing your pleasure on my holy day,
> and call the Sabbath a delight
>   and the holy day of the LORD honorable;
> if you honor it, not going your own ways,
>   or seeking your own pleasure, or talking idly;
> then you shall take delight in the LORD,
>   and I will make you ride on the heights of
>   the earth;
> I will feed you with the heritage of Jacob your father,
>   for the mouth of the LORD has spoken.
>   (58:13–14)

We can return to obeying the Lord and maintaining the fellowship while we still have breath (Lam. 3:40–41). God sees our hearts, not just our actions. He recognizes that our problem is deeper than simply not going to church or fellowshipping. We do not because our hearts do not trust him. We do not trust his provisions (so we work an extra day). We do not trust that he can restore relationships (so we hide from them). We do not trust what he says is good for us (so we scheme our own ways).

David experienced this separation from the community and it cost him dearly. Scripture emphasizes the fact that he withdrew from the community when he was not supposed to: "In the spring of the year, the time when kings go out to battle, David sent Joab, and his servants with him, and all Israel" (2 Sam. 11:1). Scripture then highlights the key problem again by saying that he alone stayed back: "But David remained at Jerusalem" (11:1). During this time alone, he coveted a man's wife, committed adultery, and murdered a man to cover it all up. It was not until he was back in fellowship that he was made aware of his sins and repented (2 Sam. 12:13).

He then penned Psalm 51, where he laments: "Create in me a clean heart, O God, and renew a right spirit within me. Cast me not away from your presence, and take not your Holy Spirit from me. Restore to me the joy of your salvation, and uphold me with a willing spirit" (vv. 10–12). Beyond the real life setting of this Psalm is the contextual one. David's prayer for individual restoration has others in view: "Then I will teach transgressors your ways, and sinners will return to you. . . . my tongue will sing aloud of your righteousness" (vv. 13–14).

Finding individual forgiveness with God leads to the edification of others. When we find forgiveness, we are able to teach others how to find it.

Many verses in the Bible emphasize that we must return to God individually and communally.

> If you return to the Almighty you will be built up. (Job 22:23)

> But when in their distress they turned to the LORD, the God of Israel, and sought him, he was found by them. (2 Chron. 15:4)

> Let us test and examine our ways,
>   and return to the LORD! (Lam. 3:40)

> Come, let us return to the LORD;
>   for he has torn us, that he may heal us;
>   he has struck us down, and he will bind us up.
> After two days he will revive us;
>   on the third day he will raise us up,
>   that we may live before him. (Hos. 6:1–2)

Repentance leads to healing, restoration, and revival.

We must also reconcile with others, not just God. A great New Testament example of this occurs when Paul had a falling out with Barnabas over John Mark (Acts 15:36–41). Paul did not want to bring John Mark along with them because he had abandoned them in an earlier missionary journey. So Paul and Barnabas separate. Nevertheless, Paul later reconciles with John Mark (Philem. 24; Col. 4:10) and values the ministry of Barnabas (1 Cor. 9:6).

A successful restoration of fellowship is not based on the amount of good deeds we do, but on God, who has mercy on such prodigal sons and daughters as us. Not only does he want us to remain in fellowship with other believers, but we are often told of the blessings that follow when we do. Jesus tells us that he is especially present at times with his gathered people, "For where two or three are gathered in my name, there am I among them" (Matt. 18:20).

At the end of the day, we must make certain that our time together is more—far more—than a pixelated message, voice on the phone, or smile at church. We must ask our community and ourselves: Is our time together real, a facade, or a dream? Are we mirroring Paul's daily concern "for all the churches" by caring about churches beyond our local vicinity (2 Cor. 11:28) and believers we have never met "face to face" (Col. 2:1–2)—their adherence to the gospel, their spiritual health, their behavior, their unity?

In certain cases, community can be a bad thing when we use it to further our own pride or create a disguise of spirituality. Perhaps we should start by asking ourselves, are we heeding Jesus's warnings against the danger of seeking human approval, acting holy to get attention, and going out of our way to be noticed (Matt. 6:1–2, 5, 16)?

Yet even with all these cautions in mind, the benefits of spending time together with others—life on life—far outweigh the risks. Close fellowship with believers reduces our troubles, maximizes our joys, helps others, meets needs, avoids heresies, fosters humility, and increases gratitude. Our hearts are less likely to become hardened. We are less apt to fall into the deceitfulness of sin.

We cannot follow Jesus well apart from God's community: the one, holy, universal church. The core of our relationships must be with believers, and the majority of our time should be spent with our spiritual family. We are one in Christ. Yet despite our need for Christian community, we are called to be great commission believers as well, which means we can't be isolated from the world. Thus, we must also spend time together with nonbelievers.

Time Together with Nonbelievers

As Christians, we acknowledge all others as never entirely "other." We do not have an "us versus them" mentality— that is, those inside versus outside the fellowship of Christ. We are all God's image-bearers, and we all have intrinsic value as God's created beings.

At the same time, Scripture reveals two categories of people: those who belong to the world and its ruler, Satan, and those who belong to God (Acts 26:18). These two classifications are explained in terms of opposites throughout the entire Bible. For example, those in darkness and those in the light; those with eternal life and those with eternal death; those who have peace with God and those who are at war with him; those who believe the truth and those who believe lies; those on the narrow path to salvation and those on the broad road to destruction. There is a profound difference between believers and nonbelievers according to God's Word. It is from this perspective that we must discern what kind of time together we can and should spend with nonbelievers.

We know from Scripture that interacting with nonbelievers is necessary—indeed, commanded and encouraged. In Scripture, wisdom is personified and shown as active— in homes and on the streets—not sitting around quietly in a church. In order to reach the uncommitted, unaware, uninterested masses with her teachings, Lady Wisdom cries out! In order to be heard above the hustle and bustle of daily life, she screams, shouts, begs, cautions, rebukes, reasons, threatens, and warns—all quite unrefined and unfashionable. But she cries out so that people will not waste their lives. Acceptance of wisdom is often equated with acceptance of God. As believers, we need to remember wisdom still calls, and we need to help nonbelievers hear her voice.

Like Lady Wisdom, we, too, should share the Word of God with as many people as possible. Our primary relationship with nonbelievers is evangelistic. The prophet Jeremiah tells us that even if he tries, he cannot stop sharing truth about God: "If I say, 'I will not mention him, or speak any more in his name,' there is in my heart as it were a burning fire shut up in my bones, and I am weary with holding it in, and I cannot" (Jer. 20:9). The prophet Daniel notes this: "And those who are wise shall shine like the brightness of the sky above; and those who turn many to righteousness, like the stars forever and ever" (Dan. 12:3). Paul writes to the Corinthians: "Woe to me if I do not preach the gospel!" (1 Cor. 9:16). Just as Jesus sent out his disciples to be among nonbelievers (Matt. 10:16–18), so he sends us (Matt. 28:19–20). He commands us to love our enemies, and not "greet only your own brothers" (Matt. 5:46–47).

At the same time, while we are loving our nonbelieving neighbors, we must always remember that they do not live under the Word of God. They do not surrender to the Spirit's leading. They do not embrace the centrality of Christ. They do not know biblical wisdom. They cannot love others or us as they ought. They cannot stop following "their own sinful desires" (Jude 16; cf. Rom 1:24ff); and sometimes, we must decline their invitations to spend time together with them (Neh. 6:2).

Declining these invites can be difficult and cause us pain. Peter writes to the churches in Asia Minor,

> For the time that is past suffices for doing what the Gentiles want to do, living in sensuality, passions, drunkenness, orgies, drinking parties, and lawless idolatry. With respect to this they are surprised when you do not join them in the same flood of debauchery, and they malign you. (1 Pet. 4:3–4)

Yet even these moments are wonderful evangelistic opportunities. Earlier in the same letter, Peter encourages us to always be ready to make a defense for the hope that lies within us (1 Pet. 3:15). This may be especially true when others ask us why we don't participate in harmful activities. Nevertheless, our best and deepest bonds can only exist in Christ and for Christ. We must not settle for cheaper relationships that are usually shallow, fickle, and short-lived.

But when we do spend time with nonbelievers, we must not expect nonbelievers to behave as we do. When we are around them, say at work or in a social situation, they may use foul language, tell off-color jokes, etc. What should our response be? Some Christians express offense at such behavior, going so far as to request that the nonbeliever refrain from such language or behavior while in his or her company. Usually, the nonbeliever finds this response offensive, judgmental, and expressive of a holier-than-thou attitude. It seems that the believer is trying to maintain a pristine atmosphere for himself while disregarding the reality of the nonbeliever's condition. Perhaps it is better to accept them as they are, where they are, rather than force them to engage in a pretense for the sake of the believer's presumed holiness. There are better ways to introduce Christ than to demand a sudden, dramatic change in behavior while in the rarefied atmosphere of a Christian when such a change does not reflect the reality of where the unbeliever is.

Consider also for a moment that our time together with believers fosters our outreach to nonbelievers. In essence, our corporate gathering is missional. It excites us to draw others in. It gives us joy when others embrace Jesus and join us for the sake of the gospel. In fact, the first thing Paul mentions in his letter to all the saints, overseers, and deacons in Philippi is that he is grateful and joyous because of their "partnership in the gospel" (Phil. 1:5).

The author of 1 John shares similar sentiments at the beginning of his letter: "That which we have seen and heard we proclaim also to you, so that you, too, may have fellowship with us; and indeed our fellowship is with the Father and with his Son Jesus Christ. And we are writing these things so that our joy may be complete" (1 John 1:3–4). Being a community of believers who share the good news of Jesus Christ with nonbelievers is one of the most glorious privileges we have and joyous things we can experience.

Granted, we do not always know who is who—that is, who is in Christ and who is not. We don't have a window enabling us to look into anyone's soul; but as Jesus said,

"Let both grow together until the harvest, and at harvest time I will tell the reapers, 'Gather the weeds first and bind them in bundles to be burned, but gather the wheat into my barn'" (Matt. 13:30). In the meantime, Jesus tells us, "Let your light shine before others, so that they may see your good works and give glory to your Father who is in heaven" (Matt. 5:16). He also lets us know how our time together with believers affects our witness: "By this all people will know that you are my disciples, if you have love for one another" (John 13:35). Unless our fellowship reflects this love, our time together is not healthy, nor is our community remarkable or influential. Thus, our time together with brothers and sisters in Christ has profound implications for our mission to go and make disciples (Matt. 28:19–20).

One method of accomplishing this mission is through planned occasions. Consider Jesus, Paul, and others going into towns for the purpose of sharing the good news of the kingdom of God. Think of missionaries like Hudson Taylor, who organized a successful effort to evangelize the interior of China.

On the other hand, we must also be on alert to share the Gospel through unplanned opportunities. Think of Philip's unplanned encounter with the Ethiopian eunuch in Acts 8, where he helped a confused reader of Scripture come to Christ. Remember when Peter and John were going about their way to pray in Acts 3, and they were interrupted by a lame beggar sitting outside the temple courts. They stopped, and Peter spoke to him "in the name of Jesus Christ of Nazareth" (v. 6). The lame man was immediately healed—leaping and praising God as one who experiences God's salvation. Consider the time in Acts 16 when Paul and Silas were praying and singing hymns to God in jail, and all of a sudden there was a great earthquake. They used this unexpected moment to remain faithful and ultimately lead a Philippian jailer and his household to Christ. Paul's later testimony helps clarify his method of staying ready for these types of spontaneous opportunities: "For though I am free from all, I have made myself a servant to all, that I might win more of them" (1 Cor. 9:19). He saw and experienced the joy of being ready at a moment's notice and winning others to Christ. The fatherless receive a father, the homeless a home. People are healed, lives are restored, names are written in the Lamb's book of life, and God is glorified.

Closer to our time period, the well-known professional baseball player turned preacher and evangelist Billy Sunday experienced such a spontaneous invitation and subsequent conversion. After grabbing a few drinks one afternoon with his teammates, they were sitting outside a local bar listening to some live music being played off in the distance. All of a sudden, a passerby invited them to come and join the Christian meeting where the music was coming from. Only Sunday stood up, went with the man, and ultimately trusted in Jesus Christ. After his conversion, and during his evangelistic ministry, he led a young man to Christ named Mordecai Ham. From there, Ham's faithful preaching of the gospel convicted another young man of his need to commit his life to Jesus Christ. That young teenage boy was Billy Graham. Praise God for such spur-of-the-moment invitations, and the God-ordained chain of events that follow.

We also need to pray, as Paul instructed the church at Colossae, for open doors and to make the most of every interaction with nonbelievers (Col. 4:2–6). We need to know our surrounding culture and engage with it purposefully. Paul quotes pagan poets when preaching in the book of Acts. He notes Corinthian slogans in his letters to Corinth. The author of Jude addresses a bookish community familiar with literature outside Scripture. All of these techniques were employed to connect with a culture and create more opportunities to share Christ in ways that were meaningful to them. Our sense of accountability to God motivates our efforts to win people to faith: "knowing the fear of the Lord, we persuade others" (2 Cor. 5:11).

Of course, these are not just new covenant concepts. Moses shared with Jethro all that the Lord had done in delivering Israel, and Jethro ends up joining the community, bringing an offering and sacrifices to God and eating with Aaron and all the elders of Israel (Exod. 18). Later, Moses invites his father-in-law, Hobab, to join the community. Although Hobab rejects the offer, Moses repeats the invitation with a more urgent plea, and Hobab agrees to follow (Num. 10). We learn later that there are decedents of Hobab in the Promised Land among the tribes of Israel (Judg. 4:11). We also see believers, like the men of Issachar, "who had understanding of the times, to know what Israel ought to do" (1 Chron. 12:32). What a powerful and important combination of cultural engagement and missional outlook. Ezekiel discusses the responsibility of Israel's watchman to warn the wicked that disaster is coming (Ezek. 33).

Whether it is in the Old or New Testament, we find the same principle: we must spend time with nonbelievers and continue sharing the truth of God's Word in love. At the same time, while the type of reactions and responses to hearing the truth are endless, Jesus did counsel us not to cast our pearls before swine (Matt. 7:6). Meaning, there are times and situations when the right thing to do is not share the spiritual and sacred things of the gospel with people who will only scorn it and have no inclination of accepting it—though much prayer and discernment is needed first (see also Matt. 10:14; 18:17; Acts 13:46; 18:6; 19:9).

As we invite nonbelievers into the community of God's people, they conform to us, not the other way around. This was true during the days of Moses. Non-Israelites who joined the community were required to adopt the rituals and rules of their new society (Num. 15:14–15). The Lord also communicated it through the prophet Jeremiah: "They shall turn to you, but you shall not turn to them" (Jer. 15:19). This principle should remain intact today (2 Cor. 6:14–7:1; 2 John 10). The important question to ask as we spend time with nonbelievers, then, is who is influencing whom?

SUMMARY

We are designed to crave and thrive in relationship with others. Sadly, Adam and Eve's disobedience broke our harmonious fellowship with God and others. Now, we live outside of Eden. Now, both of those relationships are deeply distorted. Time together can be challenging and sometimes disappointing.

Since the fall, recovering our time together in faith is the necessary antidote to perfecting those relationships and restoring this aspect of the rhythm of the Christian life. God's goal is to restore us to the holy rhythm of time alone with him and time together with others in Christ. He first did this by giving the Israelites commandments regarding the rhythm—commandments such as "you shall love your neighbor as yourself" (Lev. 19:18) and "you shall love the LORD your God with all your heart and with all your soul and with all your might" (Deut. 6:5). Afterward, God expanded the scope of possibility through the life, death, and resurrection of Jesus Christ. Through Jesus, we can be restored to fellowship with God and be in community with his children, living in the joy of life together.

The life-changing importance of spending time together with other believers has never been hypothetical. Real people took it to heart, applied it to their lives, and God blessed them! Others rejected it, and their lives were disastrous and, even worse, they experienced God's judgment. When we refuse to gather, we are doing what the Israelites often did in the wilderness. They did not trust in God, but in themselves. Yes, we individually and together are still imperfect and sinful. We are simultaneously sinners and saints. But as we have seen, it has always been God's intention for his children to spend intentional time together, and it always will be as we read about our eternal state—one with no strife, no fighting, no fear, and no distrust.

Although being united in Christ is already a present spiritual reality (Eph. 2:6; Col. 3:1–4; 1 Pet. 2:4–5), one day "we will always be with the Lord" (1 Thess. 4:17); and together as God's children, "we shall be like him, because we shall see him as he is" (1 John 3:2). As the author of Revelation concludes, "Behold, the dwelling place of God is with man. He will dwell with them, and they will be his people, and God himself will be with them as their God. But nothing unclean will ever enter it . . . but only those who are written in the Lamb's book of life" (Rev. 21:3, 27).

At this point, one might object to the idea of spending so much time in community: *I can't imagine never having a moment to myself.* Granted, if we only spend time together with others, it can be draining and discouraging. We can burn out, feel overwhelmed, or experience depression when we constantly pour into others. Jesus knew this all too well when he said to his disciples, "'Come away by yourselves to a desolate place and rest a while.' For many were coming and going, and they had no leisure even to eat" (Mark 6:31). We must spend time alone, but in the right way. To explore what "the right way" means and how we can find it, we turn now to the next chapter.

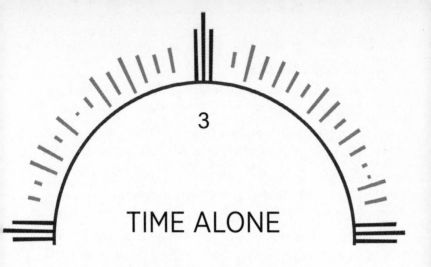

3

TIME ALONE

*Great crowds gathered to hear him and
to be healed of their infirmities. But he would withdraw
to desolate places and pray.* —Luke 5:15–16

*The day together will be unfruitful without the day alone,
both for the fellowship and for the individual.*
—Dietrich Bonhoeffer, *Life Together*

There are many benefits of spending time alone. Regular intervals of solitude allow us to reorient ourselves uninterrupted. Hearing the leaves crunch under our feet as we go on a secluded hike, walking on a desolate beach as the sand gives way under our feet, soaking in the warmth of a long bubble bath, and sitting peacefully under the night sky can all be relaxing and rejuvenating. Whether it is a mountain, beach, farm, ranch, desert, home, car, or building, we can experience peaceful periods alone without all the noise, distractions, or hustle and bustle of life that are regularly around us.

When we encounter times like these, we typically return to our normal schedule better off than before. Our communication with others usually improves. Our ability to work more efficiently and effectively soars. Our long-term enjoyment generally increases. We benefit—as do the people around us—when we pause periodically and spend time alone. This need for time alone naturally complements the ongoing rhythm that keeps our lives in balance.

At the same time, there is nothing inherently Christian or intentionally religious about those delightful reclusive times and locations. They are often occasions when we simply unplug from the commotions and diversions around us. Our brains get a chance to rest and replenish. People popularly refer to them as "a getaway," "a vacation," or "a staycation."

However, not all times alone or withdrawals from people are positive. Some people abandon their responsibilities, like a parent deserting his or her child. Others neglect their duties, like a military member who intentionally misses the boarding of a ship or an aircraft, or deployment with a unit. Still others try to escape and run away from someone or something, like a teenager running away from his or her home or an adult drifting from place to place looking to start "afresh." These types of time alone or withdrawals are negative. They give rise to failure. Weaknesses set in and these bad habits become the person's new home. Breaking the chains of these horrible habits becomes exceedingly difficult. They are like a soft bed—easy to get in to but hard to get out of.

While time alone is usually great, it is never the greatest. We may feel good for a moment, but those times are always fleeting. If we only spend time alone getting away from the noise, then we are missing God's best for us: himself. The best time alone is when we commune with God—pouring out our concerns, confessing our sins, asking for help, meditating on biblical truths, reflecting on God's beauty and majesty, expressing our gratitude, considering eternity. There is nothing more reasonable or profitable than spending time alone with our Father in heaven. Souls are awakened. Hearts are convicted. Thoughts are corrected. Burdens are lifted. Problems are solved. Eyes are enlightened. Joys are celebrated. Lives are changed.

When we spend time alone with God, we not only nourish our relationship with him but we also nourish a better life for us. Spending time alone with God pulls us away from everything that we think gives us purpose and meaning (be it our job, education, hobbies, social status, relationships, parenting) and re-centers us on the one who knows what we really need. This type of time alone is not a flight from noise. It is not to get away from the workload. It is not to have a movie-marathon-day, golf outing, or brief respite from our responsibilities. Put simply, time alone with God is a purposeful pursuit of peace.

Our problem, however, is that we often do not prioritize our private devotion with God as we should, or do not realize the full magnitude of its effects. We sometimes live as sheep wandering without a shepherd and apart from the flock. If we are honest with ourselves, it is not that we do not have the time. We all have time to do what we need to do and the same amount of time as everyone else to do it—twenty-four hours a day, seven days a week, 365 days a year. It all comes down to priorities. We invest our time in the things we value. We make sure to attend the things we prioritize the highest. Think about it. We may skip out on a hair appointment or miss a sporting event, but we will not neglect a chemo treatment or ignore a big business deal. Why? Priorities.

When we feel we do not have enough time, we should ask ourselves: Where am I spending my time? What am I making time for right now? Who or what do I love, and why?

Jesus—busier than everyone around him during extensive periods of teaching, traveling, healing, and working miracles—maintained his time alone with the Father. He never went without it. He modeled the importance of taking time apart from the daily duties of one's life to spend time alone with God.

Now, some may be tempted to think at this point that spending time alone with God is not a subject ripe for new perspectives. And in one sense, that is correct. There are no new ideas being proposed here. Rather, we are reviving old ones. We are renewing the contemporary church and ourselves in ancient Christian practices.

Most Christians know that spending time alone with God—praying, meditating, fasting, confessing, reading—is essential. But if we know it's essential, why is it not a priority? Why do we allow competing responsibilities to win out? And why does the time we do spend with

God feel inadequate? Could these thoughts reveal the real need for us to reexamine this topic? Could it be that the church's preaching and teaching has left out that the key component in our time alone with God is that it's meant to work in rhythm with our time with others?

We will unpack this more in the next chapter, but our private devotional life—including reading the Bible, prayer, intercession, fasting, meditating, solitude, journaling, confession—must be in the context of and in view toward the Christian community. We must, as Bonhoeffer put it, consider how our "hours of aloneness react upon the community. . . . either to its health or to its destruction." If we emerge from our time alone built up—expressing the fruit of the Spirit—we are simultaneously serving and strengthening the fellowship. If our personal devotions stay segregated and self-centered, we are at the same time hindering and weakening the fellowship.

Consider your thyroid gland. When it works naturally and supplies your blood stream with the right amount of two hormones, all the cells in your body can work properly. If it does not produce enough of these hormones, your entire body will suffer. The onset of an underactive thyroid may not cause noticeable symptoms. But over time, if this individual part of your body remains untreated, all of your members will suffer—perhaps even leading to obesity, infertility, joint pain, and depression. This one localized part of your neck, then, is a good illustration. It either positively or negatively contributes to the health of your whole body, just as every Christian does the body of Christ.

Bits and pieces of this concept are certainly seen in other writings, but a book-length treatment on the rhythm between the two has been nonexistent until now. What is often missed in those works is that our time alone is not solely about us or for us. All too often, because of what we've heard and read, our time alone centers around us alone: our goals, our dreams, our job, our learning, our projects, our preaching calendar, our heart, our sins, our struggles. We pray for God to guide us, bless us, and use us—all so that we can have a happier life and experience more success.

Granted, there is nothing inherently wrong with those types of prayers or desires. Indeed, we are commanded to examine ourselves, and it's entirely natural and spiritually beneficial to desire and pray for good things for ourselves. But if they are the sum total of our time alone, we have missed the mark. At a certain point, we need to take the focus off ourselves and prioritize others. Yes, even in our time alone. Remember what Jesus said: "You shall love your neighbor as yourself" (Mark 12:31). That does not only apply in the public moments, but the private ones too. We should pray for others, as we would have them pray for us.

The purpose of our time alone is bigger than us alone. If we are *only* trying to achieve a greater individual closeness to God, then we are failing our spiritual family. We are setting a bad example of being united in Christ. We are distorting the truth about corporate life. We are squandering our gifts and talents by rebelling against God's Word that calls us to edify one another. Yes, we need to drink the life-giving water of Jesus individually (John

4:10), but we cannot forget that we ingest it in the context of nourishment drawn from a communal well (John 4:6).

One key test of our time alone is how it connects to our service to others. Otherwise, spending time alone with God becomes self-serving. Private devotions about ourselves and for ourselves turn out to be self-centered and self-defeating.

We may even get to the point of thinking that our private devotional life is a valid replacement for regularly spending time in Christian community. Or we may believe our time alone with God can look however we want it to, that there is no real need for us to be in his Word for that relationship. We can reach the point where just talking to God privately is enough to maintain a relationship with him without the need for Bible reading.

We need routine solitude, but it must be in the context of life together. Our individual spiritual formation must lead to mutual edification. Our vertical relationship with God is meant to express itself horizontally in loving others.

What if Jesus had not prayed to God for Peter's faith? Satan may have sifted his faith, and Peter would not have been able to strengthen his fellow believers (Luke 22:31). Similarly, there are people who need our prayers right now, and still others who will be affected by the people for whom we pray.

Christians spend time alone with God so that we are strengthened for the benefit of the body of Christ. Paul uses the imagery of the church being a "body" for a reason. The entire body weakens if any member weakens. The entire body strengthens when any member strengthens.

Think of it like the concept behind Muscle Activation Therapy (MAT). Each muscle needs to do its part so that the body functions with maximum efficiency—being flexible, strong, and healthy. If one muscle is not doing its job, other muscles and joints have to overcompensate and work harder to offset it. The goal of MAT, then, is to identify and strengthen all the surrounding muscles that are not "firing," "triggering," or "jumpstarting" properly. It treats the causes of the pain, injury, or tightness, not the symptoms.

In the same way, just as the strength or weakness of one muscle leads to the effectiveness or strain of others, the beneficial or detrimental time alone of an individual Christian can help or hurt the body of Christ.

A key benefit of our time alone is that we return to our time together with something to give from what we received rather than returning to others from a place of emptiness. We need time alone so that we can reengage our spouse, bless our kids, serve others, and influence our communities. We often enter our time alone with personal insecurities, but exit with confidence in Christ. We come with hardened hearts, but leave with them softened by the Holy Spirit. We arrive with our will, but depart with God's will. During our time alone, God shapes our hearts in part so that we can connect with and bless others who need gospel hope.

Indeed, we are dangerous to our community and others if we do not spend time alone with God regularly. Why? We will be seeking from others what only God can provide us—true love, complete approval, ultimate happiness, pure joy, authentic identity. Without God, our priorities will be messed up. Our loves will be disoriented. Our motives will be wrong. Then, when others cannot give us what only God can, we will become disappointed, frustrated, and burned out. At that point, we will take all those emotions out on others—perhaps via gossip, slander, and manipulation.

Only God can give us the wisdom to respond in kindness, peace in times of pain, hope when all seems lost, and our purpose in an otherwise meaningless world. The community alone can never fully meet our needs. We also need time alone with God.

Time Alone with God

Our best life includes frequent time alone with God. There is a genuine sense of spiritual empowerment when we commune with him. Scripture amply shows this. As we consider a few Scriptural examples, observe and reflect on what all these stories have in common.

Wonderfully in Sync

So what does the Bible say about spending time alone with God? Let me again draw your attention to a few passages from both the Old and New Testaments.

Old Testament

In the book of Genesis, we see that God's covenant people can trust him to give them guidance and success when they are walking in obedience. These moments of guidance and success often come when they are spending time alone with God. As Isaac, Abraham's promised son, spends time alone meditating in a field, God sends him his future wife, Rebekah. We may be tempted to think this is just a coincidence, but it is not. From Scripture, we know that God sovereignly orchestrated every detail while Isaac was walking in obedience—even the fact that Isaac was ultimately comforted after his mother's death because Rebekah became his wife (Gen. 24:63).

Then later, during another one of Isaac's times alone, he offered up a prayer of intercession for his wife because she was unable to conceive a child. The Lord immediately grants his prayer on her behalf and she becomes pregnant (Gen. 25:21). What sheer relief he must have felt knowing God was with him, providing for his every need during those difficult times.

After God freed the people of Israel from slavery in Egypt, and rescued them from the Egyptian army via the Red Sea, they camped in the wilderness at the base of Mount Sinai. During their time there, the people sinned by worshipping a golden calf. Their evil actions prompted Moses to spend time alone with God in order to intercede on their behalf (Exod. 32:11). Good thing he did. Because of his private prayers to God, we see that "the LORD relented from the disaster that he had spoken of bringing on the people" (Exod. 32:14). God longs to see an individual stand in the gap, interceding on behalf of an entire community like Moses (Ps. 106:23; cf. Ezek. 22:30–31).

Shortly thereafter, while spending time with the Lord, Moses asks him, "Please show me your glory" (Exod. 33:18). What a simple, yet profound prayer coming from someone who was purposefully pursuing peace. After dealing with such "stiff-necked" people, Moses probably felt exhausted and lonely. So he pressed into his time alone with God by seeking to know him more deeply and intimately. The Lord replies, "I will make all my goodness pass before you" (v. 19).

So powerful was his individual time with God, that when he returned to the community, they all saw Moses's face literally glowing (Exod. 34:30). While only Moses saw God pass by him, all the Israelites were able to see God's ways. Moses was changed, *and* the community was blessed (Ps. 103:7).

Hannah "was deeply distressed" because the Lord closed her womb and another woman made fun of her because of it. Imagine how she felt seeing other women feeding their newborns, helping their toddlers take their first steps, or walking around town with their numerous kids. She probably wondered, *Why me? Have I done something wrong? What is wrong with me? Why doesn't this other woman care that my heart is tearing apart inside of me?*

Had Hannah let her emotions flow without bringing them to the Lord, who knows what would have happened. Perhaps she would have become distant, indifferent, and cold. Thankfully, she spent time alone with God. She shed her tears before him (1 Sam. 1:10). She shared the secrets of her heart. As a result, she was blessed: "Hannah conceived and bore a son, and she called his name Samuel, for she said, 'I have asked for him from the LORD'" (1 Sam. 1:20).

Reflecting on Hannah's life, it makes even more sense that her son, Samuel, a prophet of God to Israel, also became a person who often spent time alone with the Lord praying and interceding for others. She likely passed along her devotional habits to her son by modeling them in her life. For instance, after establishing the first king of Israel due to the sinful request of the people, Samuel told them that he would not sin against the Lord by stopping to intercede for them (1 Sam. 12:23). He would continue focusing on and serving others via his prayer life. And those were not just his words but also his actions. Later, when he learned that the king he established, King Saul, offended God by disobeying his command, "he cried to the LORD all night" (1 Sam. 15:11). Through and through, Samuel was known as a man who spent time alone with God, and God answered his prayers (Ps. 99:6).

The book of Psalms gives us some of the best examples of how we should live out the life-changing habit of spending time alone with God. There are many indications that the Psalmist planned his time alone with God and encouraged others to do the same. He says to God in the future tense, "In the morning, O LORD, you will hear my voice" (Ps. 5:3 NASB). He states elsewhere that he begins his mornings in prayer (Ps. 88:13; 119:147). He shares how he longs for the night watches of meditation—those still, quiet, and contemplative times often found between sunset and 10 p.m.; 10 p.m. to 2 a.m.; 2 a.m. to 6 a.m. (Ps. 63:6; 119:148). He also instructs others to think and meditate during the night hours: "ponder in your own hearts on your beds, and be silent" (Ps. 4:4). Perhaps nursing mothers know these times best, even if they are only half-awake.

The Psalmist reminds us repeatedly that God is not distant. He is always available—in the temple or anywhere—for those who seek to spend time with him (Ps. 91:1). He also anticipates the blessings that flow from intimate time alone with the Lord, such as joy (Ps. 4:7), divine favor and protection (Ps. 5:12), and healing from pain and suffering (Ps. 30:11). What a blessed life! Through his time alone with God, the Psalmist experiences God's loving-kindness and steadfastness. The Psalmist tells us, "in [God's] presence there is fullness of joy" (Ps. 16:11), and we see those qualities in how he experiences God during his time alone with him. "When the cares of my heart are many," the Psalmist shares, "your consolations cheer my soul" (Ps. 94:19). God is not loved without reward, even though he should never be loved for the rewards.

The familiar story of Daniel being saved from the lions' den provides another vivid example of the need for and blessings from spending time alone with God. Because of the intensity of the situation, we may miss the events leading up to the miracle. We may overlook the real beauty of Daniel's private devotional life.

King Darius had issued a decree that no one could pray to any god or man for thirty days or they would be thrown into the lions' den. Daniel faithfully disobeyed the king's ordinance. Regardless of the cost, he continued getting down on his knees three times a day to spend time in prayer with God and praising him (Dan. 6:10). He knew that something mattered more than his own life—his daily relationship with God.

Daniel's view of his time alone with God ought to move us to reconsider our own convictions. Would we be willing to die before we would give up our time alone with God? Imagine never seeing your family and friends again; never finishing what you have already started; never accomplishing your ultimate goals. With those stark realities in front of him, Daniel still decided to remain faithful.

Daniel was ultimately punished, according to the decree, by being cast into the den of lions. But the Lord delivered him. How sweet and invigorating that must have felt seeing God's hand on his life.

As Daniel's life continued, he maintained his built-in routine of spending time before the Lord for his own sake and for the sake others (9:20). Then we see and learn something about his time alone that is out of this world. An angel, named Gabriel, comes to Daniel and tells him that "a word went out" when he started praying, "for you are greatly loved" (9:23). Imagine that! Daniel had a great reputation in heaven because of his time alone, and the angel Gabriel was sent to give him a word and understanding—opening up doors of thought and insight.

Daniel's entire life shows us the authentic realness of living life in the rhythm God ordained, which far surpasses all other ways of living. We, too, ought to pause periodically and contemplate on our reputation in heaven. Do we have one similar to Daniel? If not, why not?

The prophet Habakkuk provides us with another magnificent example of living in sync. When he was struggling with his surrounding circumstances, wondering why so much evil was going on around him, he cried out to God. He did not try to drown his sorrows in alcohol or wallow in self-pity. He spent time alone with God, asking questions and sharing his frustrations—knocking at the throne of grace while faithfully manning his post. He essentially asked God the same types of questions we all ask at times: *God, are you seeing all this injustice? Why don't you seem to care? What is the purpose of all this?*

In the midst of sharing his complaints, he even challenges God's initial response that harder times were still on the horizon for Habakkuk. Just imagine if God responded to you that way, *If you think it is tough now, just wait. It's about to get worse.* Eventually, Habakkuk's attitude changes from distress to comfort. He ends up feeling refreshed and renewed again. After pouring out his heart in the presence of God, he was restored to harmony. How freeing it is to be completely vulnerable and transparent—finding contentment and peace when connected with God. Listen to his final words as they form one of the most powerful statements of faith recorded in all of Scripture:

> Though the fig tree should not blossom,
>> nor fruit be on the vines,
> the produce of the olive fail
>> and the fields yield no food,
> the flock be cut off from the fold
>> and there be no herd in the stalls,
> yet I will rejoice in the LORD;
>> I will take joy in the God of my salvation.
> GOD, the Lord, is my strength;
>> he makes my feet like the deer's;
>> he makes me tread on my high places.
> (Hab. 3:17–19)

Stripped of everything else in life, we can never be deprived of our relationship with God. We are never alone or abandoned. We are always heard and recognized.

Habakkuk's time alone with God even ends on a musical note, "with stringed instruments" (Hab. 3:19).

New Testament

The life of Jesus provides us with the best model of time alone with God. It was part of his regular routine. He saw the need to withdraw from the crowds and spend time with his heavenly Father his entire life, not just at horrific times like his trial and crucifixion. Jesus spent time alone with God as recorded in the Gospel of Luke, for instance, during times of success, times of stress, key decisions, periods of anguish (5:16; 6:12; 9:18, 28ff; 11:1; 22:41–45; 23:34, 46). The location and time varied, but the practice never did. Jesus frequently withdrew to lonely places to spend time with God.

Ordinary, faithful people in the Gospels also had life-changing encounters with God when they were alone in his presence. When the priest Zechariah was alone with God in the temple, he was given the message about having a son, who would "make ready for the Lord a people prepared" (Luke 1:17). This son was John the Baptist, who would later baptize Jesus.

The apostles spent time alone with God. Peter shares that he was alone in the city of Joppa praying when he saw a vision (Acts 11:5) that ultimately led to the salvation of an entire household of Gentiles (Acts 11:14–15). Paul's time alone often led to miracles and blessings for him and others. It was the Lord who stood near Paul and encouraged him in between tough times with people (Acts 23:11). When Paul was left alone toward the end of his life, he emphasized God's presence and power in a letter he wrote to Timothy. "All deserted me," he writes, "But the Lord stood by me and strengthened me" (2 Tim. 4:16–17). After John was banished to the island of Patmos, he received the prophecy we now call the book of Revelation when he was alone one Sunday (Rev. 1:10). The apostles' lives were marked by time alone with God and how it connected to others.

This brief survey reveals something central about the Christian life: when believers spend time alone with God, blessings flow to them and through them to others. Couples meet. Prayers are answered. Disaster is averted. Confusion vanishes. Effective intercession occurs. Joy ensues. Divine favor is obtained. Souls are cheered. Deliverance happens. Questions are answered. Music is played. Divine messages arrive. Miracles occur. Hope is found. Strength builds. Salvation comes. God is glorified.

The infinite wonders of God's grace pour over us as we spend time with him—warming our hearts, filling our souls, and preparing us for life with others.

Painfully out of Sync

Sadly, though, we get off course from time to time. We do not consistently spend time alone with God, or if we do, we do not spend it as we ought or in faith. Like Jeshurun, we at times abandon God, pursue the things of this world, and trample his grace under our feet (Deut. 32:18). Like Israel, we occasionally get to the point of refusing to pay attention, turning a rebellious shoulder, and being obstinate (Zech. 7:11). Some completely ignore his instructions (Matt. 7:26) and go the way of Satan, saying, "I am, and there is no one besides me" (Isa. 47:10). We essentially set ourselves up as our own gods, pursuing our own goals and doing only what we want, thus disregarding God's will. Still others "have a zeal for God, but not according to knowledge," and therefore their belief amounts to nothing (Rom. 10:1–4).

When any of these attitudes begin to infect our lives, we become out of touch with reality like the wicked, who "flee when no one pursues" (Prov. 28:1). When we fail at the altar in our relationship with God, we also fail in the field with others, like Cain did with Abel (Gen. 4). Or we end up sitting alone by ourselves, like Jonah, in the belly of despair that could have been avoided (Jon. 3:17). No wonder these men felt disconnected from God: they stepped out of rhythm. Sin replaced God's rhythm with their rhythm. It switched God-centeredness with self-centeredness. This selfish disposition is what Paul talks about when he writes that in the last days "people will be lovers of self" (2 Tim. 3:2). Such people are anti-God, and "they will not get very far" (v. 9) because they have no intimate relationship with God, even though they are successful in the community.

Stark contrasts exist between how someone's life goes when he or she is living within the rhythm and when he or she is living outside it. In the heart of sinners, the rhythm of the Christian life is replaced with the rhythm of themselves. They base their life on an arrhythmic pattern. It is as if they have spiritual atrial fibrillation. The good news, however, is that God is willing to forgive us in Christ and restore all our wasted time.

Hopefully Re-synced

As Malachi asked when the Lord urged his people to return to him, we, too, wonder, "How shall we return?" (Mal. 3:7). After slipping into habits that crowd out time spent with God, how do we find our way back into that intimate relationship? Put simply, we fight the disease of pride with the cure of humility. We must prioritize, plan, and preserve time alone with God. We do this by choosing a daily time to step away from our frantic pace. We spend that time engaging with God through prayer, reading his Word, thinking deeply about who God is and who we are, what he has done for us and others through the cross, and what he is leading us and others to do in response.

We cannot live on our own little islands apart from him, even for a short time. It only perpetuates a vicious cycle: separation breeds more separation. Even momentary drifting apart is dangerous and detrimental in our relationship with God.

Thankfully, the Holy Spirit gives us internal warning bells to draw us back to God. When the barren Rebekah finally conceived after her husband's prayer, she felt such wild turmoil within her womb that she was alarmed. There were thoughts in her head as she was listening to herself. Perhaps she was paralyzed with fear—wondering if something was wrong with the babies, imagining if she would have a miscarriage, thinking she might go into labor early. Filled with such anxiety, she went to the Lord for discernment. She asked, "Why is this happening to me?" (Gen. 25:22).

God graciously answered her and brought clarity to the situation. He told her about the twins' struggle that was going on inside of her, "Two nations are in your womb" (v. 23). With that word from God, Rebekah was comforted and successfully gave birth to the twins. We also need to do as Rebekah did: "So she went to inquire of the Lord" (v. 22).

According to the Gospel of Matthew, Joseph, Mary's betrothed, experienced similar distress when he learned that Mary was pregnant. No doubt, he felt numb, as if the whole world just came crashing down on him. He probably stood speechless, with his future flashing before his eyes—seeing the shame that would cover him and the bad reputation that would follow him. Left to himself, without divine guidance, Joseph "resolved to divorce her quietly" (Matt. 1:19). His mind was made up. Nevertheless, he did not divorce her because of the divine message he received. He trusted in God's guidance over his own thoughts and feelings.

In the book of Acts, Peter was "inwardly perplexed as to what the vision that he had seen might mean" (10:17). As a Jew following Jewish dietary practices (Lev. 11 and Deut. 14), Peter could not imagine eating prohibited foods as the vision portrayed and commanded. But as he continued his time alone, "the Spirit said to him, 'Behold, three men are looking for you. Rise and go down and accompany them without hesitation, for I have sent them'" (10:19–20). Praise God for his extended time alone! From there, Peter's time with these men illuminated God's message in the vision that the gospel was not to be hoarded by the Jews but shared with the Gentiles. Peter then shared the Good News with the Gentiles, and witnessed the out-pouring of the Holy Spirit on them.

In the end, we must *speak* a stronger faith to ourselves like the godly saints in Scripture did—recalling verses of Scripture, praying as the Spirit leads, asking pointed questions (Ps. 42:5; 43:5; 103:1–2; Lam. 3:21)—instead of *listening* to ourselves. We need to strengthen ourselves, as David did, by taking courage in our faith-based relationship with God (1 Sam. 30:6). We must "work out your own salvation with fear and trembling," as Paul commanded (Phil. 2:12–13). We should do as the prodigal son did "when he came to his senses," having realized that he sinned against *both God and others*: repent and go back to our Father (Luke 15:17–21). We ought to sit at the feet of Jesus as Mary chose to do (Luke 10:38–42). We need to meditate on "whatever is true, whatever is honorable, whatever is just, whatever is pure, whatever is lovely, whatever is commendable . . . and the God of peace will be with you" (Phil. 4:8–9). This is not just a mental practice or intellectual exercise, but a spiritual orientation of our will and religious affections (Col. 3:2).

In our day, John R. W. Stott, the author, evangelist, and church leader, exemplified this well—how someone's time alone with God could make such a radical difference in this world. Ranked among the one hundred most influential people in the world according to *Time* magazine in 2005, Stott exercised discipline over his schedule. He maintained a steady diet of undistracted time alone with God for over fifty years. His time allotments just for study and reading consisted of one hour a day, one three-hour period a week, one entire day a month, and one full week a year.

During his time alone, he would fill his mind with Scripture. He would meditate on God's promises and see how they applied to him. He would read and study as one on a scavenger hunt—searching for a list of ways to articulate, defend, and live out the Christian faith. He would hide the Word in his heart so that he would be able to see and understand his daily activities with others correctly. After listening (via the Bible) and speaking (via prayer) to God, he returned to others with a more focused mind and heart—moved by God's majesty, freed from earthly anxieties, and grateful for the privilege of being one of God's children.

The time alone aspect of the rhythm fueled Stott's communal life, which manifested itself through his powerful and extensive ministry to millions around the world. He embraced the rhythm of the Christian life and lived it wholeheartedly—allowing his time alone with God and time together with others to work in tandem to glorify God.

SUMMARY

This chapter was intentionally shorter than the previous chapter. The calculated contrast was designed to draw attention to the fact that Scripture exhibits the same disproportion. More verses deal with time together as opposed to time alone because this is how life works: most of our waking hours are spent with people, not alone. Yet most of us gauge our spiritual life primarily by our individual devotional practices.

Through our brief reflection on spending time alone, several key points surfaced. God placed in us the need to spend time alone with him. If we follow his plan for our lives, which includes regularly spending time with him in solitude, real life-change happens. We become content. We fulfill our purpose. We live abundant lives.

On the contrary, when we insist on marching to our own beat, the opposite happens. We remain discontent. We do not fulfill our purpose. We waste our lives.

We saw the real and present danger in thinking that our time alone can be fruitful without participating in time together. Isolation cripples. It is a flower that grows in the devil's garden. We tend to overvalue individual peace. We often embrace the myth of self-sufficiency. We allow certain behaviors in our lives—self-righteousness, blame shifting, complacency, jealousy, gossiping, manipulation, guilt tripping—to go unnoticed or unchecked by most, if not all. Living in such a way alienates us from God and other people and misses the beautiful design God gave us in Christian community.

We should practice solitude, therefore, only insofar as it is not an obstacle to time together. The goal of solitude is not merely self-awareness. It is not only to be by ourselves, or even with God. Its purpose is the pursuit of peace with God and others. It is about the individual transformation that takes place so we can live and participate fully in community. Personal devotion to God fosters communal integration in the body of Christ. What does it look like? How can we balance our time alone with God and time together with others? What precisely is the rhythm of the Christian life?

The answers lie ahead. To the next chapter we turn.

THE RHYTHM

*[Jesus] appointed twelve (whom he also named apostles)
so that they might be with him and he might send
them out to preach.* —Mark 3:14; emphasis added

*One who wants fellowship without solitude plunges
into the void of words and feelings, and one who seeks
solitude without fellowship perishes in the abyss of vanity,
self-infatuation, and despair.* —Dietrich Bonhoeffer, *Life Together*

God created us to connect with him *and* others—not one *or* the other. He chooses to have an intimate relationship with us both individually and communally. We are to understand our lives in relation to both. We are to live perennially as people standing before God and connected to others. This interlocking interchange—alternating between time alone with God and time together with others—constitutes the rhythm of the Christian life.

This rhythm has nurtured believers and their believing communities for centuries as they listened and responded to the signs of their time. This reciprocal ebb and flow of spending time alone in God's presence and then returning to time spent with people is foundational for living a full life. This timeless back and forth movement expresses what is universally valid for every believer.

Sadly, believers and churches today have largely neglected the rhythm of the Christian life. Some have a constant desire to be with people; others desire the opposite. Some people run from being alone; others are uncomfortable being around others. Some do everything to find noise and distractions; others cringe at the idea of commotion. Few really contemplate the interplay between these two connected aspects of Christian living. As a result, our time alone remains unrelated to the broader body of Christ. And our time together doesn't feed into our time alone, or it becomes something we do simply because we are required to as a member of a church.

At least two reasons contribute to why this is the case. The first reason relates to the common myth that we can practice our faith however we want to, as long as we perform certain core activities, even if it excludes the church community or ignores time with God. This line of reasoning stems from a general lack of attention given to the rhythm of the Christian life and cultivates individualism.

We rush to talk about the derived components of the rhythm, known as the spiritual disciplines, and occasionally examine our group times, but rarely are the rhythm and component parts tied together and fleshed out in tandem. The absence (or minimal mention) of their continuity is seen in popular literature today. The focus of the spiritual disciplines has become mostly (or solely) about how they benefit *you*; how they draw *you* closer to God; how they help *you* overcome certain issues; how they provide *you* peace and comfort. But the Christian life is not about *you*.

Most books and resources—certainly not all, but most—divide the rhythm and separate the disciplines in order to explain them. The authors only point out, for instance, that Jesus pursued time alone with God in order to encourage us to go and do the same. While both points are true—Jesus did and we should—this overly simplistic approach strips those moments from their surrounding context. We miss the real gravity and magnificence of them, thereby diminishing their thrust. Jesus's individual times with God the Father were always in the midst of and with view toward his time with others. Scripture intentionally shows the intended flow between the two and how they are meant to complement each other.

A second reason seems to surface when we over-privatize and hyper-individualize many passages in the Bible. An important fact obscured in English Bible translations is that almost all the second-person pronouns and commands in the epistles are plural. Paul was writing to *you all* or *y'all*, not to *you* individualistically, which is how we tend to interpret them when we read individually. "Work out your own salvation with fear and trembling" is not simply a command to you individually (Phil. 2:12). The "your own" is plural, and the corporate directive of working out our salvation is in the context of a Christian community.

Similarly, the charge for us to "put on the whole armor of God" in Ephesians 6 is not meant to be understood as the armor you put on every day as a single soldier going out to face individual spiritual attacks (though there may be some extended implications for that). Rather, the truth that Paul conveys is that we are all to suit up together as a united front going out into battle in unison. As we stand together, we advance together.

The main point in all this is that by offering some simple, even helpful categories to think through the Christian life, a false dichotomy has arisen between our individual lives with God and corporate lives with other believers. This widespread mentality operative among churches and churchgoers has led to a fragmented and unrhythmic Christian life, especially in how we understand many verses in the Bible and apply them to our lives. As a result, we experience less unity and focus almost exclusively on our own individual needs. What should we do about it?

God's prescription for us is to embrace the rhythm of the Christian life in Christ. We need to investigate, appreciate, and apply the rhythm of the Christian life anew so we can do what Jesus instructed his disciples to do: "He said to them, 'Come away by yourselves to a desolate place and rest a while.' For many were coming and going, and they had no leisure even to eat" (Mark 6:31).

The rhythm of the Christian life is the place where these extremes—time alone and time together—meet. The rhythm reduces remoteness from God and others, and curtails plunging into constant community that tends to exclude time with God. This is not a peripheral matter but a central one, for Christ died so that we might be reconciled with God *and* each other, as well as live life abundantly. Yes, the gospel reaches us personally and individually, one sheep at a time (Matt. 18:12). But the gospel also places us into a community, as one flock, under one shepherd (John 10:16).

Let us also consider for a moment that the author of Proverbs instructs us to "find favor and good success in the sight of God *and* man" (Prov. 3:4; italics added). Reuben and Gad understood this when they decided not to neglect their military responsibilities "to the Lord *and* to Israel" during the conquest of Canaan (Num. 32:22; italics added). Samuel demonstrated this as a boy as he "continued to grow both in stature and in favor with the Lord *and also* with man" (1 Sam. 2:26; italics added).

Luke shares how Jesus exemplified this: "Jesus increased in wisdom and in stature and in favor with God *and* man" (Luke 2:52; italics added). Paul endeavored to do the same: "I always take pains to have a clear conscience toward God *and* man" (Acts 24:16; italics added). He also tells us that life in the kingdom of God involves serving Jesus in a way that "is acceptable to God *and* approved by men" (Rom. 14:18; italics added). Peter similarly instructs all of us: "Honor everyone. Love the brotherhood. Fear God. Honor the emperor" (1 Pet. 2:17). These two pairs of four distinct commands really encompass just two categories: God and others.

It is *not* enough to say (as true as it is) that we should spend time alone with God and time together with others. We must also emphasize the rhythm between the two and how they accompany each other. We must focus on "why" we are doing each activity and what they involve. We will not become holy or whole by ourselves, or by way of others, but by both.

Whatever issues might confuse us about what the Bible teaches, the rhythm of the Christian life ought not to be one of them. The relationship between our time alone and time together in Scripture is clear, as we will see next.

The Rhyme and Reason for the Rhythm

To understand the rhyme and reason for the rhythm, let's first consider some commonalities in the following four illustrations.

Musicians

Musicians who are part of an ensemble—be it an orchestra, marching band, jazz combo, or rock band—must practice on their own and during group rehearsal. Individual practice is always done with the whole group in mind and how all the musicians fit into the ensemble when they return. During a rehearsal, musicians learn how they may need to adjust their approach to make sure they fit in properly. Then, each musician returns to his or her individual practicing to hone these adjustments.

Assuming they have the right song for the right venue, the anticipated result is a majestic performance for the world to hear. If an instrument or vocalist misses an entrance, undershoots a high note, plays in the wrong key, or adds an additional note, it can result in an epic failure for the whole group. The ensemble's success depends greatly on the individual and collective activities of each musician.

Of course, a performance of a piece of music involves more than just each musician playing his own part as if it were an island within the broad stream of the composition. In a sense, each part interacts with the other parts in ways that would not work well if an individual performer did not also know more than his or her own part. In other words, the parts reinforce each other, either melodically or harmonically, and create something much more complex sounding than if each musician only knew and played his or her own notes at the right time.

Actors and Actresses

Actors and actresses memorize and practice their individual parts of the script so that when the entire cast comes together for the rehearsal, it goes well with the director. When it is time to perform, they hear, "Action!" Whether it is a live or recorded performance, the audience will quickly see how both the alone and group times went. If one actor dries (i.e., forgets their lines) or does not act his or her part well, then the whole performance could be jeopardized and everyone humiliated.

Athletes

Athletes playing team sports understand that the season will rise or fall depending on how each player hones his or her individual skills off the field so that when the team comes together on the field, they perform well together. Both players and coaches know there is no way to get in enough repetitions during group practice to perfect each individual's skills that are needed to compete at the highest level. Only newer, less experienced coaches think talented individuals win games and seasons. The best coaches recruit players that are coachable team players, who make everyone around them play better. They know that when a teammate breaks a rule of the game, the whole team is penalized and may lose as a result. They win or lose as a team, but how each player spends time alone preparing is critical.

Soldiers

Soldiers are typically held to high physical fitness standards. While much of this is accomplished through physical training activities as a unit, these standards cannot be met by relying on the unit training activities alone. If the individuals are not training on their own against the required standard, they will eventually fall behind. If they fall behind, the entire unit suffers and has to work harder. Indeed, they are collectively only as strong as their weakest individual link.

At the same time, when it comes time to test, individual scores improve when they are tested with others present. Especially on cardiovascular activities like running, individuals perform better when others are performing the same routine around them than if they were on the track alone. As each soldier improves, so does the strength of the unit—and vice versa.

Each one of these examples contains several key elements related to the rhythm we have been discussing. Both time alone and time together are intimately connected and are necessary for overall success. Time alone fosters or hinders time together, and time together facilitates or impedes time alone.

It is critical to note that even if every individual does well, and the entire group unites harmoniously, they may all still collapse because they played the wrong song, staged the wrong performance, arrived at the wrong location, or joined the wrong forces. That is why there is always someone ultimately in charge of making all the final decisions—the conductor, director, coach, or commander-in-chief.

It's much the same in our lives as Christians. Each one of us bears responsibility for the strengthening or weakening of our church community, and our church community either fosters or hinders our individual growth. Everything we do alone affects the church, and everything we do with others affects our time alone. One person can spoil the fellowship, and bad company can corrupt a person's good morals.

Just as orchestras have conductors, teams have coaches, actors have directors, and soldiers have commanders, we have God, "who is over all and through all and in all" (Eph. 4:6); and everything is in his capable and loving hands.

The essential rhythm that makes life best is time alone with God and time together with others. You cannot have one without the other for long without a problem. But we understand these interlocking concepts so loosely that it often gets in the way of understanding and applying the rhythm so that it leads to our best life. To capture the heartbeat of the rhythm, we must connect the pulses, consider the spiritual disciplines and our spiritual gifting, and examine it all in action.

Connecting the Pulses

Although our relationship with God is personal, it is not private—literally or figuratively. We called a royal priesthood of believers in Scripture (and royalty is never private), and there is a clear interplay between each believer and his or her believing community. This interlocking interaction is reciprocal. Our time alone affects our community and our community affects our time alone.

Biblically, we see this across the pages of Scripture. People would often spend time first in God's presence before going out with others. Let's explore again the Old and New Testaments for a few examples.

Old Testament

Moses's individual burning bush experience was not for self-enjoyment, but for his time together with others (Exod. 3:16). Aaron and his sons first spent time alone with God when they were ordained before going out among the community (Lev. 8:33). Ezra individually studied God's Law and applied it to his life, and then went to teach it to others communally (Ezra 7:10). The Psalmist states his individual trust in God alone (not just *the* Lord, but *my* Lord), while maintaining close fellowship with and delighting in God's worshipping community: "I say to the LORD, 'You are my Lord; I have no good apart from you.' As for the saints in the land, they are the excellent ones, in whom is all my delight" (Ps. 16:2–3).

Repeatedly, the Psalmist individually prays for the Lord to intervene in his life, while also anticipating the opportunity to praise him for it communally: "How long,

O Lord, will you look on? Rescue me from their destruction, my precious life from the lions! I will thank you in the great congregation; in the mighty throng I will praise you" (Ps. 35:17–18).

As the psalm continues, we see that the vindication of one person is worthy of the praise of all: "Let those who delight in my righteousness shout for joy and be glad and say evermore, 'Great is the LORD, who delights in the welfare of his servant!'" (v. 27).

When God delivers the Psalmist out of deep trouble, there is public praise (Ps. 40:1–3). His praise causes others to rejoice. Compare the beginning and end of Psalm 69, where the individual request and subsequent deliverance shifts to a communal revitalization focus:

> Save me, O God!
> > For the waters have come up to my neck. (v. 1)

> When the humble see it they will be glad;
> > you who seek God, let your hearts revive. (v. 32)

His praise ought to encourage others who are seeking God. His individual cries to God, "Make haste, O God, to deliver me! O LORD, make haste to help me!" as in Psalm 70:1, include exclamations for others, "May all who seek you rejoice and be glad in you! May those who love your salvation say evermore, 'God is great!'" (v. 4). He wants God to answer his prayer so that others can declare the Lord's greatness. His relief does not come simply by the destruction of his enemies, but by the community's experience of gladness. Even his prayers for others, such as the one for a specific leader in Psalm 72, are offered so that all will live well.

In the book of Jeremiah, during one of the prophet's personal prayers to God, he complains about his situation and lot in life. He reminds God of the suffering he has had to endure, of his loneliness, and of the lack of pleasure he finds in his work. Though he lives an upright life, everyone mocks him—not everyone in the world, but people who deem themselves to be descendants of Abraham and worshippers of God.

When God responds, we read: "The LORD said, 'Have I not set you free for their good?'" (Jer. 15:11). God turns Jeremiah's focus off himself and back onto others. The very people that mock Jeremiah and from whom he feels alienated are the same ones God calls him to minister to; and God promises that he will provide him the strength to deal with their mockery. Jeremiah's life confirms that he maintained the rhythm—continually spending time with them and with God, even offering up their prayer requests during his time alone with God (21:1–6; 42:1–6).

New Testament

As we turn to the New Testament, we see this same interplay between time alone and time together. In the Sermon on the Mount, Jesus says that if we individually go to offer a gift at the altar and remember that we are not reconciled with another believer communally, then we should leave our individual time of giving and prioritize our communal time to become reconciled with each other (Matt. 5:23–24). As he teaches us to pray, we learn that the model prayer is never "my" daily bread, but always "our" daily bread (Matt. 6:11). He follows that up by telling us that as we forgive others communally, God forgives us individually (Matt. 6:14–15). Later in the Gospel of Matthew, Jesus talks to the disciples about individual graces and communal forgiveness in the context of helping people via teaching and healing: "You received [individually] without paying; give [communally] without pay" (Matt. 10:8).

Jesus also stood up in a synagogue to let the community know that the Spirit of the Lord was upon him, not for personal pleasure but for the benefit of others (Luke 4:18). Jesus tells us that just as an individual lamp is to give light to all in the house, our individual light is to shine before others so that they may ultimately give glory to God (Matt. 5:15–16). Jesus's call to follow him as an individual (Matt. 9:9) always leads to being sent among others (Matt. 10:5). Immediately after Jesus "went up on the mountain by himself to pray" (Matt. 14:23), he went to others, his disciples, walking on the sea, saying, "Take heart; it is I. Do not be afraid" (14:27).

We also see this pulsating movement in the life of a widow of great age. In the Gospel of Luke, the author highlights her private devotional life because it prepared her for her public proclamation:

> She did not depart from the temple, worshiping with fasting and prayer night and day. And coming up at that very hour she began to give thanks to God and to speak of him to all who were waiting for the redemption of Jerusalem. (Luke 2:37–38)

In another New Testament book, we see the rhythm pulsating when a group of Jews in Berea "received the word" that Paul and Silas shared with them in the synagogue communally. Then they also searched "the Scriptures daily to see if these things were so" (Acts 17:11). What they received during their time together drove them back to the text individually. We also learn that overseers are commanded: "Pay careful attention to yourselves and to all the flock" (Acts 20:28). Again, we see the two-fold rhythm. Spiritual leaders are to concentrate on their own relationship with God *and* the spiritual condition of those under their care.

In several other New Testament books, we see the same phenomenon. We read how Paul aims to win Christ's approval (2 Cor. 5:9) *and* human acceptance for the advance of the gospel (2 Cor. 6:13). He goes on to powerfully state his love for others, "I will most gladly spend and be spent for your souls" (2 Cor. 12:15). We are also told to keep our focus on both Jesus *and* other godly believers:

> Let us run with endurance the race that is set before us, looking to Jesus, the founder and perfecter of our faith. (Heb. 12:1–2)

> Keep your eyes on those who walk according to the example you have in us. (Phil. 3:17)

We are to carefully observe and imitate both Christ and those mimicking him. We must develop personal relationships with others, along with our personal relationship with God.

The entire letter to the Galatians provides us another great example of the rhythm between individual time with God and time together with the community. We see that God called Paul individually so that he would preach Jesus to others communally (Gal. 1:15–16). We read that the only thing that counts is individual faith expressing itself through communal love (Gal. 5:6). We learn that the purpose of our freedom—our liberation from sin, false gods, the law—is to serve others through love (Gal. 5:13). This specific type of love necessitates a mutual concern for others in our community, including some extremely difficult and needy people. We are to support, help, and restore each other, as well as watch out for ourselves individually, so that we can fulfill the law, which is carrying each other's burdens as we balance carrying our own. We must support and help each other communally, while remembering that we will each stand before God individually (Gal. 6:1–2).

All in all, there is flexibility within the rhythm, but the rhythm itself must remain intact. Scripture makes it clear that everything is for God's glory *and* the benefit of others (2 Cor. 5:13). In Christ, Paul commands: "Let each of you look not only to his own interests, *but also* to the interests of others" (Phil. 2:4; italics added). In spite of Paul's sin, Jesus individually strengthened him so that Paul could achieve certain results communally (1 Tim. 1:12). Paul tells Timothy to practice what he is sharing "so that all may see your progress." And as Timothy keeps a close watch on himself and "on the teaching," he is commanded to "Persist in this, for by so doing you will save both yourself *and* your hearers" (1 Tim. 4:16; italics added).

We also, like Paul, ought to persevere and endure all kinds of individual hardships for the sake of other believers. He writes, "Therefore I endure everything for the sake of the elect, that they also may obtain the salvation that is in Christ Jesus with eternal glory" (2 Tim. 2:10).

To be sure, God does at times speak directly to individuals concerning themselves. Jesus even gave a poignant example in a parable about a rich guy who hoarded all his wealth: "But God said to him, 'Fool! This night your soul is required of you . . .'" (Luke 12:20). Yet also like this parable, the individual insights are often still meant to illuminate other areas in our lives as they relate to communal living: ". . . and the things you have prepared, whose will they be?" (Luke 12:20). The reason is that, by and large, our lives are communal. Our time alone usually looks toward our time together with others. The real test of the effectiveness of our time alone is often our time together. Simultaneously, the test of our time together can be measured during our time alone.

A Brief Word on Spiritual Gifts and Spiritual Disciplines

Spiritual gifts are essentially the special abilities or roles—such as evangelism, giving, administration, and prophecy—God has given us individually to serve the body of Christ communally. By definition, the rhythm of the Christian life is at the core of all such gifting. Indeed, we exercise our spiritual gifts to strengthen others.

In Romans 12:3–8, we see that God uniquely gifts individuals to enable them to contribute positive benefits corporately. Paul, writing elsewhere about the use of spiritual gifts, makes a similar statement that every gift we have received individually should be used for the building up of all believers communally (1 Cor. 14:26). The author of 1 Peter specifically tells his audience that their individual spiritual gifts are to be used to serve others communally, not just themselves individually (1 Pet. 4:10).

If our gifting does not join the rhythmic dance, it is off beat. We are merely drawing attention to ourselves or seeking self-advancement. When the Holy Spirit gives certain people the gift of giving, for example, their generosity should be without strings attached. Otherwise, they are not giving to the community; they are buying status for themselves. A hidden agenda is at play, perhaps to be a powerbroker at church or to receive greater name recognition.

With all spiritual gifting, we improve our individual gifting through time alone with God and with the intent of supporting our Christian community. Throughout Scripture, we are reminded of our inability to be self-sufficient. We are unable to perfectly embody the Christian life alone. We need the gifts of others, and they need ours. It is by exercising our gifts in the body of Christ that we hone them and make them stronger, receiving feedback and encouragement as we use them.

If we turn to reflect for a moment on the spiritual disciplines that foster our spiritual growth, we see the same thing. Our individual spiritual disciplines, such as fasting, and our corporate spiritual disciplines, such as worship, are intimately connected and work in tandem to glorify God. They set each other in motion, like Newton's cradle or when one billiard ball striking another sets the second one in motion.

Consider the discipline of prayer. As we study the topic of prayer in the Bible, we discover that a person's prayer life is deeply personal and considerably communal. Whenever we pray as individuals, we are told to have a communal mindset (Mark 11:25; cf. Matt. 5:44–45).

This fact is seen frequently throughout the Bible, especially in the Psalms, where we find the mingling of individual and communal voices. The singular and plural first-person pronouns ("I/me" and "we/us") are interchangeable in many places because the person's (prayer) life is so strongly connected to the community. The individual's experience of God's forgiveness, healing, salvation, and blessing is in the context of how God has forgiven, healed, saved, and blessed the community. As an individual is delivered from troubles and experiences God's goodness, all should rejoice and experience these blessings themselves. God strengthens individuals for the community and the community for individuals. God is at once involved at both the individual level and the communal level (Ps. 118:19–21, 25).

The Psalmist often shares his personal experiences and praises in order to summon others to experience and praise God. Look at Psalm 34: "I will bless the LORD at all times" immediately shifts to "magnify the LORD with me, and let us exalt his name together!" (vv. 1, 3). The psalms were not written merely for the king's time alone with God apart from the congregation (e.g., see Psalms 25 and 28). The king represented the people, and all that concerned him concerned the people. What was true for

King David, including his concerns and requests for deliverance, could be applied to himself and the nation.

The Psalmist may speak as one person among all of Israel, yet he speaks as one who is in close fellowship with them. Look how Psalm 111 opens: "Praise the LORD! I will give thanks to the LORD with my whole heart, in the company of the upright, in the congregation" (v. 1). Or take a look at how the individual prayer of Psalm 106 relates the one to the many. The merger between the individual and the community is already complete by verses 4–5 (italics added):

> Remember *me*, O LORD, when you show favor to *your people*;
> help *me* when you save *them*,
> that *I* may look upon the prosperity of *your chosen ones*,
> that *I* may rejoice in the gladness of *your nation*,
> that *I* may glory *with your inheritance*.

Personal terms broaden to include others. The author's voice becomes our voice. You can see the same phenomenon elsewhere, such as Lamentations 5 when the individual laments become remarkably communal. This mingling of voices is another testimony in Scripture that singular and plural aspects converge in the rhythm of the Christian life.

We also see Jesus regularly praying for people. He even prays for their time with still other people—understanding their interconnectedness. Here are two of the rare glimpses Scripture provides us into the specifics of Jesus's prayer life:

> *I have prayed for you* that your faith may not fail. And when you have turned again, strengthen your brothers. (Luke 22:32; italics added)

> *I am praying for them.* . . . Keep them in your name . . . that they may be one, even as we are one. . . . I do not ask for these only, but *also for those who will believe* in me through their word, that they may all be one. (John 17:9, 11, 20–21; italics added)

Yes, our time alone behind closed doors is always necessary and to be encouraged: "When you pray, go into your room and shut the door and pray to your Father who is in secret. And your Father who sees in secret will reward you" (Matt. 6:6). But those times ought to be filled with prayers for others, as they were for Jesus.

Scriptural examples of and requests for intercession on behalf of all people are widespread in the New Testament (Rom. 15:30; Eph. 6:18; 1 Thess. 5:25; 1 Tim. 2:1–4; James 5:16). The author of the book of Hebrews notices this individual unity with the community when he writes, "Jesus offered up prayers *and* supplications" (Heb. 5:7; italics added). In fact, we learn that Jesus still makes intercession for us (Heb. 7:25; Rom. 8:34).

In the same way, we cannot fully understand the significance of our personal experiences of God's grace via our spiritual gifting or the spiritual disciplines apart from God's actions as they relate to his people. Our personal experiences connect with the community, and our communal experiences connect with our personal experiences. God does not relate simply to individuals. Our significance is situated in our relationship with the community.

Whatever spiritual gift we have or spiritual discipline we practice in our life, we must realize that there is a foundational interconnectedness and reciprocal effect at play in our time together with others. We cannot gauge our personal piety simply by what we do in private—for we can all be pretty pious when we are by ourselves. Our common commitment to Christ ensures that we do not merely perform as individuals. Our common commitment and purpose includes specific individual gifts, talents, and callings, but all of them connect to one another and combine to make one body.

Wonderfully in Sync

Although God made us all in his image, we are different in so many ways. Some people run from being alone; others are uncomfortable being around others. Some people do everything to find noise and distractions; others cringe at the idea. Some people wish they were more connected; others are well connected but never stop to think about the depth of those friendships. Regardless of circumstances or personality types, all God's people should align themselves with God's purpose, plan, and pattern for their lives, not prioritize their culture's principles, proposals, and preferences. The saints of old knew this, as we see in Scripture. Let's look at a few accounts in the Old Testament and then in the New Testament.

Old Testament

In the book of Genesis, Abraham tasks his servant to find a wife for his son Isaac (Gen. 24). The focus of this passage is on the servant's faithfulness in following God's guidance. The importance of the mission motivated him, not its difficulty or ease. The responsibility drove Abraham's servant to spend time alone with God, praying for a successful mission (vv. 12–14). God answered his prayer by sending Rebekah to be the wife of Isaac. God also blessed his time with Laban and Bethuel as they extended hospitality and approved his request to take Rebekah back with him. All this caused him to bow his head and worship the Lord (vv. 26, 52).

The life of Moses displays the same pattern. After "Moses went up to God" alone on the mountain (Exod. 19:3), he "came and called the elders of the people" and told them what the Lord shared with him during his time alone (v. 7). From there, Moses went back to the Lord to share their response, and the Lord directed him back to the people (v. 10). "So Moses went down from the mountain to the people," as God said, "and consecrated the people" (v. 14). And in a beautiful culmination, Moses, Aaron and his sons, and the seventy elders see God and enjoy a covenant meal together on the mountain (24:9–11).

The book of Numbers contains still other examples from Moses's life because he was accustomed to living in the rhythm. For instance, his time together with others was draining and demanding, as people were complaining and weeping, and it drove him back to his time alone with God (Num. 11). His time together with his people allowed him to realize what he needed most—God's help and intervention (v. 14). Then God told him to go back to the people, and he did (v. 24). The outcome was the appointment of seventy elders to assist Moses in bearing the burden of the people (v. 17). A few chapters later, the entire congregation is complaining again, even after God had threatened to destroy them because of their continual whining. This moves Moses to spend time alone with God to intercede for the people. The Lord then forgives the people according to Moses's prayer (Num. 14:20).

New Testament

The New Testament opens up with a story about how Joseph's time alone was impacted by time together with his fiancée Mary. In fact, it changed his entire outlook on life and his future. During their time together, he received some severely disturbing news regarding his virgin fiancée being pregnant. The communication drove him to spend time alone to "consider these things" (Matt. 1:20). During his time alone, he receives a much-needed divine message, which prompted him to faithfully follow through with the Lord's perfect plan.

Two chapters later, John the Baptist baptized Jesus (Matt. 3). After his time together with John the Baptist, the Spirit led Jesus into the wilderness, where he spent time alone with the Father for forty days and forty nights (Matt. 4). It becomes immediately evident that Jesus was able to resist all the Devil's temptations (something no one has ever been able to do perfectly!) because he was fasting, focusing, and feasting on his personal relationship with God. Though physically weak, he was at his strongest spiritually, and sin was averted. After his extended time alone, which included divine testing, Jesus returns to Galilee and launches his three-year public ministry: "From that time Jesus began to preach, saying, 'Repent, for the kingdom of heaven is at hand'" (4:17).

As the story continues, we read that Jesus chose the twelve disciples "that they might *be with him* and he might *send them out* to preach" (Mark 3:14; italics added). They were each called to him individually, shaped by his presence and teaching, and then sent out to make disciples communally. What Jesus modeled, he mandated. It was Jesus's "custom" to go to the synagogue with others (Luke 4:16), just as it was his "custom" to pray (Luke 22:39). As believers in Christ, we, too, are simultaneously one person (called to spend time with God) and the one elected community of God (called to spend time together in Christ and make disciples).

After the death of John the Baptist, we see one of the most explicit narratives in all of the Gospels regarding the rhythm of the Christian life:

> The apostles returned to Jesus and told him
> all that they had done and taught. And he
> said to them, "Come away by yourselves to a
> desolate place and rest a while." For many were
> coming and going, and they had no leisure
> even to eat. And they went away in the boat to
> a desolate place by themselves. Now many saw
> them going and recognized them, and they
> ran there on foot from all the towns and got
> there ahead of them. When he went ashore he

saw a great crowd, and he had compassion on
them, because they were like sheep without a
shepherd. And he began to teach them many
things. (Mark 6:30–34)

Just when they planned and expected to have some time
alone, another time together with others stared them
in the face. And Jesus had compassion and prioritized
others over himself. The disciples urged Jesus to dismiss
the great crowd, but instead he miraculously fed them.
Immediately after feeding them, he dismissed the crowd
and "went up on the mountain to pray" (v. 46).

Our serving others flows into our need to be cared for
apart from other people (Mark 3:13–19; 9:2). We periodically withdraw from people to focus on our relationship
with God and purposefully pursue peace.

All four Gospels show Jesus spending time alone with
God before, during, and after time together with others:
before he calls the apostles, when he blesses God for the
multiplication of food, when he heals the deaf mute, when
he raises Lazarus, before he asks for Peter's confession
of faith, when he teaches the disciples how to pray, after
the disciples return from their mission, when he blesses
the little children, when he prays for Peter, during the
last supper, during the meal at Emmaus, as the Passion
was approaching, in agony in the garden, and while on
the cross.

Among other things, Jesus's time alone with God
kept him focused on what just happened, was happening, or was about to happen regarding his time together
with others. By abiding in God's love, wisdom, and power,

Jesus was able to bear much fruit with others. His time together was an overflow of his time alone.

Besides seeing Jesus live out the rhythm of the Christian life in the narrative accounts, it was also embedded in his teachings for us to read about. In the Gospel of John, for instance, he gives us the powerful metaphor of the vine and the branches (15:1–17). We must first abide (or dwell) in our relationship with Jesus, and live out our new identity in Christ in the relationships we have with one another. "These things I command you," he concludes, "so that you will love one another" (John 15:17). The type of love we are to have for one another is the same love by which he loves us: "By this we know love, that he laid down his life for us, and we ought to lay down our lives for the brothers" (1 John 3:16). Our source and ability to love others communally comes from our intimately abiding relationship with God.

As the Lord caused the church to grow in the book of Acts, we see the rhythm of the Christian life played out repeatedly. Ananias receives a vision from God when he is alone. The message is to go meet with a man named Saul. Ananias obeys the Lord. He finds Saul and lays hands on him. Saul regains his sight, is filled with the Holy Spirit, and is baptized (Acts 9:10–19).

After this, a devout man of prayer named Cornelius is praying alone when he receives a message from God telling him to send some men to get the Apostle Peter. In the meantime, Peter is spending time alone with God in prayer when he receives a message from God preparing him for his time together with those who were sent by Cornelius.

This back-and-forth interplay between the times alone of multiple individuals and the gathering of several people ends with the first clear Gentile conversion and reception of the Holy Spirit in the book of Acts (Acts 10). God broke Peter of his deep-seated racial intolerance. Peter learned that God shows no favoritism. The uniting of Jews and Gentiles had begun. Jesus opened the door to all people.

Later, in one of Paul's letters, Paul tells Timothy, "Keep a close watch on yourself and on the teaching. Persist in this, for by so doing you will save both yourself and your hearers" (1 Tim. 4:16). His personal piety and doctrinal integrity were to be maintained not only for personal benefits but also for communal benefit. His individual pattern of life and reading of Scripture held promise for both him and others. God's desire for others became Timothy's desire for others.

While we are temporary residents on earth, Peter tells us that our whole pattern of life toward others should be different because we each call upon God as our Father (1 Pet. 1:17). He states this shortly before providing the living metaphor of stones and a house. Peter says each of us is like a living stone, and all of us together can be assembled to create a strong, spiritual house (1 Pet. 2:4–5). Only for a moment does he focus attention on our individual status as single stones. But even then, we are not pictured as alone or separated from others. We are simultaneously seen as part of God's great temple. Although we remain individuals, we are identified together with others as collective stones in one spiritual house. All of us draw near to God individually, while also being built up communally. That is why Peter immediately shifts the focus from us as individuals to us as a community. The real focus is on our corporate identity. Even the success of our individual prayers throughout the day are linked to our interactions with others and the way we foster love for one another (1 Pet. 4:7–8).

The New Testament church seems to have assumed that Christians focused their thoughts and actions on others. Like the early church, we are instructed to spend time together regularly, even daily. Consider these two commands from the author of Hebrews:

> Exhort one another every day. (Heb. 3:13)

> Let us consider how to stir up one another to
> love and good works, not neglecting to meet
> together, as is the habit of some. (Heb. 10:24–25)

The reasons Scripture gives us for why we must daily encourage each other are because, otherwise, we may "fall away from the living God" or "be hardened by the deceitfulness of sin" (Heb. 3:12–13). We cannot neglect meeting together, because otherwise we will not experience the full assurance of our faith (Heb. 10:19–22). We cannot abandon each other, for God never abandons us (Ps. 9:9–10; 37:27–28).

Perhaps some of us have experienced this principle of "in sync-ness" at the church level. Maybe we attended a church that identified it as a core value. They did a good job of providing us valid opportunities for togetherness—worship assemblies, focused classes, small groups. They continually encouraged us to spend time alone with

God—via teaching or even with send-home devotional material. They constantly connected and modeled the two aspects for us, while reminding us that we do not just relate to each other but are related—by faith in Christ.

For others, maybe the in sync-ness occurred at the small-group level. Maybe we had a close-knit community that truly loved, served, and encouraged one another in Christ. We lived life together as we ought—keeping each other accountable when together, interceding for one another when spending time alone with God, and bearing witness to the gospel together with our nonbelieving neighbors.

Either way, we probably do not need to pile up additional examples in support of the harmonious flow and strong connection between our time alone with God and time spent with one another, or of the glorious benefits we experience when we live in the rhythm of the Christian life. Both are evident in Scripture and can be seen today. But perhaps we do need to take a quick glance at what can happen when we do not live in the rhythm of the Christian life—when we are painfully out of sync and do not experience our best life.

Painfully out of Sync

Sometimes we live life off tempo. We forfeit peace, hope, and joy. We drift away from the biblical picture of the gospel, which balances for us the rhythm of the Christian life—the personal and the interpersonal, the private and the communal, the one and the many, the individual and the community. We separate God's call on our lives to live in the rhythm. We slip out of the rhythm because of things like selfishness ("I don't have time"), laziness ("I'll get to it later"), and rebellion ("I don't have to!"). When this happens, life is not best, because we live in direct disobedience to God. Without the rhythm of the Christian life, our faith lacks focus and stability. When we neglect it, we are more vulnerable to Satan's attacks, the lies and lures of this world, and the sin that so often entangles us.

Again, as we open our Bibles, examples abound. Moses maintained the rhythm even when his culture did not. He regularly went up the mountain to meet alone with God, and the community knew it. When he did not return to them as they expected (Exod. 32:1), the people "corrupted themselves" (32:7). They sought to replace the leadership they feared they had lost in Moses with an idol—the infamous golden calf. By prioritizing their own principles, proposals, and preferences, it led to the corruption of a whole community. The entire group succumbed to temptation, departing from the rhythm, and Moses had to intercede for them again lest God destroy them.

After a man in the Israelite army named Achan secretly took for himself specifically forbidden spoil in a battle against the Canaanites, Joshua's army was unexpectedly defeated in their next battle. Though only one man sinned, Scripture says that "Israel" broke faith (Josh. 7:10). God viewed Achan's individual sin as if the whole community committed the trespass. What was done in secret apart from the community's knowledge was brought to light, and the guilt and punishment was transferred to the whole group. By personally indulging in sin, he weakened the entire nation.

This account helps underscore a main aspect of the rhythm of the Christian life: everything we do (or do not do) affects both us individually and the group communally—for better or worse. Maintaining the health of the community goes all the way down to the individual level, just as Paul says in the New Testament: "If one member suffers, all suffer together; if one member is honored, all rejoice together" (1 Cor. 12:26). In fact, Paul rebukes all the Corinthians for the private sin of one person (1 Cor. 5:4–6). He lets them know that they will not thrive while such a disgrace is attached to them.

The principle is as true today as in biblical times. The whole church is infected by one private sin, just like your entire body is affected if you have a sinus infection. When any brother or sister behaves immorally, shame covers us all. One person's moral nosedive can rob an entire people of purity and holiness. Corporate guilt and individual responsibility are connected before God.

Therefore, a congregation cannot be indifferent toward the sin(s) of its individual members. There is always collateral damage. Sad examples of this abound today in the many instances of leaders who have failed to live in sexual purity. Their individual sin has sent shrapnel through the body of Christ, just like the fragments of a bomb fly in all directions when it explodes.

This interlocking interplay is what Jesus, Paul, and others convey in the New Testament. They recognize when it is absent, misappropriated, or broken. They know the result is always unpleasant, disastrous, or both. And their hearts break when they see people preferring to fly off with the world instead of resting in God's rhythm.

Moreover, when God forgives us individually, he expects us to forgive others communally. In one of Jesus's parables, the servant the master forgave of an enormous debt immediately went out and demanded payment from a debtor who owed him little more than pocket change in comparison. When we do something similar, we are acting as a "wicked servant" (Matt. 18:32–35). If we give an offering to God individually, but are negligent in inter-personal matters, Jesus could say to us what he once said to others: "Woe to you, scribes and Pharisees, hypocrites! For you tithe mint and dill and cumin, and have neglected the weightier matters of the law: justice and mercy and faithfulness. These you ought to have done, without neglecting the others" (Matt. 23:23).

Our time alone is either weakening or strengthening us as a whole, and our time together is either increasing or decreasing our individual faith. This thought should be sobering to us, knowing that we could be dragging down our whole family of faith, or they may be pulling us down with them.

What we need, then, is a radical change—not in doctrine or theology, but in practice and lifestyle. We have to put our individual talents to work communally. If we do not, instead of hearing those most precious words, "Well done, good and faithful servant," we will hear, "You wicked and slothful servant!" (Matt. 25:14–30). We must realize that the things we do to others are as if we are doing them to God. We should not be shocked or confused when final judgment comes and we see that whatever we did to others was as if we did them to God—the two are inter-connected (Matt. 25:40).

It is not even enough to ask: What do I do? Where do I do it? How do I do it? We must also ask: To what end do I do it? What is the purpose?

A prime example of how time alone can become utterly self-centered and self-righteous, instead of other-focused and humble, is found in the parable Jesus gave about the two men who went into the temple to pray to God (Luke 18:9–14). The first one exalted himself over others, being confident in his own righteousness as a religious leader. The second one was a humble tax collector, maintaining an attitude of personal unworthiness before God. It is appalling to imagine that our views toward others can be so skewed even as we are in the presence of God, like the Pharisee in this parable. Instead, we should mimic the other man, the tax collector, who said, "God, be merciful to me, a sinner!" At this point in Luke's narrative, Jesus is about to die and he doesn't want people to be like the religious ruler.

These narcissistic attitudes were not just illustrations in parables. They occurred in real life. Just as Israel often refused to hear anything that would call their choices into question, Jesus encountered similar types of responses from various people. Even some religious leaders pridefully refused to hear anything that would call their convictions into question (Luke 6:6–11).

A breakdown of the rhythm can occur at any moment and negatively affect us and those around us. It can happen during communion, when we fail to wait for one another and do not demonstrate normal Christian hospitality (1 Cor. 11:33–34). It can hinder our individual prayers, as when we mistreat our spouses (1 Pet. 3:7). It can come about while we are giving, when we first need to leave the altar and go reconcile with someone (Matt. 5:23–24). When our teaching is not based on sound knowledge, it can lead to a truncated view of God's way (Acts 18:26). The failures are not always fatal, but they are never favorable.

Many nations, people, and churches have fallen because they were deceived into thinking that the best life could be found somewhere outside the rhythm of the Christian life. The nation of Israel tried it. Achan tried it. The Pharisees tried it. The Corinthian church tried it. All of them failed and experienced God's judgment. On top of that, the weight of carrying those burdens around was not worth it. Regular and noticeable pain occurs when we live outside of God's commanded rhythm.

Hopefully Re-synced

Instead of waiting until our circumstances reduce us to helplessness, we ought to return to the rhythm of the Christian life at the first sign of being out of sync. By means of the Spirit, we must immediately break out of any destructive, self-centered pattern so that we can prayerfully re-sync with God's intended rhythm. How, then, do we return to this glorious, timeless, and demanding rhythm? Let us consider how David, Elijah, and Peter fell out of rhythm and then returned to it.

As we saw in Chapter Two, David was not perfect. Yes, he valiantly fought Goliath, wrote worshipful psalms, and displayed godly perseverance under Saul. But he also coveted another man's wife, committed adultery, lied to cover up his sins, and had a man murdered—all in the span of one chapter (2 Sam. 11). His choice to march to his own beat brought judgment upon himself and others, and it also blocked the grace God would have supplied if David had not stepped out of God's rhythm for his life. Hear afresh what the Lord told him after he fell away:

> I anointed you king over Israel, and I delivered you out of the hand of Saul. And I gave you your master's house and your master's wives into your arms and gave you the house of Israel and of Judah. And if this were too little, I would add to you as much more. (2 Sam. 12:7–8)

If David felt that the Lord had not already given him enough, all David had to do was spend time alone with God and make his requests known. In return, the Lord would have given him "much more." But instead, David took matters into his own hands. In turn, he failed miserably and suffered the consequences. Take a moment to seriously reflect on the lost opportunity of what God might have done in David's life had David not chosen the path he did.

We, too, rarely contemplate the squandered opportunities of our sin; what God might have provided us had we not turned down the wrong road. But hopefully among the community of trusted friends we presumably developed when we were living in the rhythm, someone would confront us like Nathan did to David. David's repentance before God and return to the rhythm was a direct result of his time together with another believer. If we also repent, God promises to forgive us, and he can still use us.

Elijah was a high-profile prophet. He caused rain to stop for over three years, successfully prayed for a boy's life to return to him, and defeated some false prophets by calling down fire from heaven. But when Elijah heard that King Ahab got angry and his wife Jezebel vowed to put Elijah to death, Elijah ran away into the wilderness. Although he was exhausted and frustrated, seemingly ready to live in isolation apart from everyone else, we see that God would not allow him to neglect meeting together with others. God would not allow Elijah to remain in utter isolation nor to believe that he alone was righteous. It was time for Elijah to take the focus off himself, realize there were other godly believers like him, and return to the rhythm (1 Kings 19).

One of the best examples of returning to the rhythm is the Apostle Peter. Peter was in strong fellowship with Jesus and his followers, but broke from the fellowship during Jesus's trial and crucifixion. On the night Jesus was arrested, Peter—among Jesus's innermost circle of friends and the first disciple to identify Jesus as the Messiah— denied even knowing Jesus on three separate occasions when people accused him of being one of Jesus's followers. Upon realizing what he had done, Peter broke down and wept bitterly. Peter later sought and received full restoration when he spent time with Jesus on the Sea of Galilee (John 21:15–17).

Peter's failure did not forever disqualify him, but it did necessitate a 180-degree return back to the rhythm of the Christian life. Subsequent to his time alone with Jesus, Peter gathered with the eleven other disciples and addressed a crowd of people in Jerusalem, and about three thousand people were saved (Acts 2:41).

We cannot assume we are living in the rhythm simply because we are doing certain activities, like praying, studying our Bibles, and spending time in fellowship. We may even wonder at times, *Why is this not working for me?* If we wonder why we drop to our knees and pray, open up our Bibles and study, show up to church and fellowship, and it is not working for us, it is probably because we are merely performing the activities and not imitating the entire lifestyle God desires and deserves.

Imagine if a young baseball player buys all the right equipment and then learns to mimic the correct arm motion and bat swing of the best professional baseball player in the world. That alone will not make him a professional ballplayer one day or even produce the best results on the field if he does not also emulate their entire athletic lifestyle—practicing multiple hours every day, maintaining a strict diet, and exercising appropriately year-round. We, too, must regiment our entire spiritual life, as Jesus did his. Not just in major moments or at specific times, but in everything all the time.

How do we live in this rhythm while maintaining a proper perspective?

Living in the Rhythm

Life ebbs and flows. As it does, the rhythm of the Christian life provides us stability. It stabilizes our multifaceted, constantly changing lives. It provides us safety and security in its dependability. When we live in the rhythm of the Christian life, we have a firm foundation that we can stand on as we anticipate future uncertainty. We experience more peace amidst our doubts and struggles.

For clarity's sake, notice that we are not trying to "find" the rhythm, but "live" in the rhythm. The good news is that God delights in helping us live in the rhythm, keeping a steady beat like the pendulum of a metronome swinging back and forth in tempo. That is why he has already set the rhythm for us. We do not have to drum it up on our own, or establish our own rhythm of spirituality. The only thing we must do is get into the rhythm God ordained, and find the best ways to stay there.

To be sure, there are numerous rhythms in life, including relational, vocational, and spiritual. Finding our tempo in the midst of them is important. People of different callings and circumstances, with their individual needs, will find various rhythms in life that help them— dieting, exercising, sleeping, socializing. Even spiritually, some people use acronyms to provide a type of rhythm to help themselves or teach others to make decisions, pray, read, or understand theological concepts (WWJD, CATS, FEAST, TULIP). But those rhythms and tempos are not what we are focusing on here.

We are seeking to live out and live within *the* rhythm God has already designed for us and intends for us to embrace—the one in which we move back and forth between drawing nearer to God and to one another in Christ. This back-and-forth complement, or two-beat rhythm of the Christian life, is not one lived in the safety of withdrawing from the world, but one fully engaged in it. Any aspect of our understanding of the rhythm that dilutes the centrality of Christ, or diminishes our calling to make disciples of all peoples, is off.

We are also not attempting to standardize precisely how, when, or where the rhythm is manifested in our lives. Those factors will change greatly depending on our life stage, location, and physical ability. Styles and patterns will vary, but the divine rhythm remains fixed. Whether you spend time alone in the morning, afternoon, or night, inside or outside, is not the point. It is about living in the regularity of the rhythm, regardless of those minor details.

Trying to give proportionate time and effort to every aspect of our life is unrealistic. It would be overwhelming and pointless to try to keep everything in our life—children, spouse, work, house, yard, family, friendships, church, recreation, and more—in perfect balance. This typically leads to exhaustion, frustration, and malfunction. But at the same time, we must guard against living in the extremes. Imagine a man or woman working so hard to make a living for his or her family that he or she neglects time with them. Or even a person so engaged in church work that he or she doesn't take time for personal reflection or for family.

A godly woman who lived out the rhythmic balance in her life—maintaining a passion for spending time alone with God and achieving positive results within her family and the community—was Sarah Edwards. She was the wife of Puritan pastor and theologian Jonathan Edwards. But long before they met, she was already living according to the rhythm of the Christian life. The rhythm naturally continued into her marriage and with her eleven children, as they would all spend time alone and together on both a scheduled and spontaneous basis. The community often praised her for how she so successfully managed all the affairs of the house, reared such wonderfully well-behaved children, and supported her husband in all his endeavors. There is no doubt that her unwavering devotion to God and commitment to others fostered such accomplishments. Her legacy endures to this day.

The beauty, benefits, and effectiveness are not found in either time alone or time with others, but in the rhythm between the two. Centered in Christ, the ongoing rhythm fosters rest and service. Imagine your heart. Its only rest is in the rhythm of action. While you are alive, your heart never stops. Yes, it rests, but only between beats. A combination of both motion and rest is required for the heart to work as God intended. In the same way, we rest in the rhythm of action. This timeless rhythm flows into the different seasons of our lives. God blesses this rhythm. God provides the rest—breaks from action, as well as whatever is lacking.

When we live in rhythm, we owe it to the blood of Jesus and the power of the Holy Spirit. Just as a withered hand cannot reach out unless God permits it, living in the rhythm of the Christian life is not something we achieve or do on our own. We lack the ability. We lack the resources. Rather, we can only live in the rhythm by means of the Holy Spirit—the omnipotent Spirit of God whom God placed in us the moment we believed in Christ. Otherwise, we will falter and fail.

Discerning whether we are living in the rhythm of the Christian life includes examining ourselves frequently before God and regularly asking trusted believers around us. Some of us cannot stand to rest. Others wish they could rest more. Some tend to be more individualistic, while others fear going against the consensus. Nevertheless, the fact is, we *all* need *both* time alone *and* time together. Our lives cannot always be lived on a high with others or in seclusion away from people. Those extremes are not realistic. If we end up constructing a false version of the rhythm, reality will eventually destroy it, and we will lapse into arrhythmia.

We will not live in the rhythm by accident; though, over time it should become second nature. Living in the rhythm of the Christian life is only possible where there is obedience. Hearts must change, not just schedules. Living in the rhythm of the Christian life is hardly ever easy, but it is always best. It is vital for the body of Christ and for us individually.

When we live in the rhythm, we are standing on common ground. We are doing what all mature believers do across the Christian tradition. The ecumenical importance of finding this time-honored, solid footing allows us to further embrace and listen to one another across denominational lines—making sure that we do not just glut our own dogma or keep the log in our eye.

In the end, we need to live in the rhythm of the Christian life, not just understand it. We must guard against being sound in our understanding while soundly asleep in our living it. We must not be too rigid or too inflexible. Jesus healed on the Sabbath, for example, showing us that human well-being takes precedence over rest or rules. There are dangers when we focus so much on one aspect that we forget the other, or even focus exclusively on the rhythm. The best way forward is to focus on Jesus and obey all that he commanded. Put simply, we are seeking Christlikeness. In doing so, we will become a person who lives in the rhythm as Jesus did.

SUMMARY

Is it possible to draw clear lessons from studying all the biblical accounts we have explored in this chapter? The sheer number of stories and qualifications resist any easy categorization. Here are a few clear observations for us to consider, drawn from Scripture.

Our quick glance at the rhythm of the Christian life revealed that people experience their best life when they live in it. Missions succeed. Forgiveness happens. Blessings flow. Divine intervention transpires. Help follows. Faithfulness flourishes. Holiness increases. Nourishment comes. Love abounds. Churches grow. People rejoice. Health restores. Salvation occurs. Baptisms emerge. Assurance takes place.

On the other hand, when people choose to march to their own beat, their lives are a mess. Hearts harden. Sin occurs. Destruction comes. Guilt is sensed. Disgrace is felt. Shame is experienced. Faith weakens. Pain increases. Confusion appears. Communion is condemned. Prayers are hindered. Giving is impeded. Truth is curtailed. Failure arrives. Burdens linger. Grief persists.

When understood biblically, the rhythm of the Christian life is the shortcut to godliness, success, blessings, and divine favor. Believers receive great grace when they embrace it. Prophets, priests, kings, mothers, wives, and daughters all sought the same treasure in life: harmony with God and others. Moses modeled it before the

Hebrew people, Jesus displayed it for the disciples, and Paul practiced it within the early church.

The whole life of a believer, no matter when or in what context, ought to be given over to the ministry of loving God and others—just as Christ did. We need God and each other jointly. The interlocking back-and-forth movement between our time alone with God and time together with others fulfills our calling.

Indeed, there are some inherent dangers in all this. We may pursue life together on our terms and within limits we control, where "life together" really just becomes "life apart" (indeed, separatist and schismatic). A great example of this in Jesus's day would have been the Qumran community. This Jewish sect believed they were the true remnant of Israel. They physically separated themselves from the Temple in Jerusalem and lived together in the Judean wilderness, determining who was "in" and who was "out" of God's ultimate plan of redemption. Their "life together" was really just "life apart."

We, too, may create our own little communities apart from the broader body of Christ. We may ignore the rhythm and choose to do things the way we have always done them. We may settle into a life that only cares for comfort. We may slip out of the rhythm without returning to it. We may do it with the wrong motives or not in faith. We may artificially perform certain actions without embracing the entire lifestyle it requires. We may even mistake keeping the status quo for stability.

The key point is that, ultimately, time alone with God and time together with others should not to be separate categories. One of the problems is that we compartmentalize everything instead of seeing one, unified whole working together. Rather than thinking of time with God and time with others as two separate activities, we should visualize them as the opposite points in the movement of a single pendulum. Scripture never divides or confuses the two. For that reason, we desperately need a paradigm shift. We need holistic expressions of God's brilliant design for us.

The rhythm of the Christian life is always active; and when lived thoroughly, it is life-giving for all. It helps prevent (or drastically reduces the amount of) failures, anxieties, and conflicts. It clearly expresses and successfully strengthens our walk with God and ministry effectiveness. It is also good news for the world, as humanity is able to see a foretaste of the new heavens and the new earth.

We must now ask, finally: How do we make the rhythm of the Christian life a reality in our lives? What steps can we take toward ensuring we live in the rhythm that God expresses in Scripture?

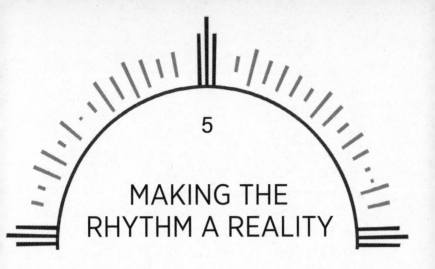

5

MAKING THE
RHYTHM A REALITY

*Only take care, and keep your soul diligently, lest you forget
the things that your eyes have seen, and lest they depart from
your heart all the days of your life.* —Deuteronomy 4:9

*The most experienced psychologist or observer of human
nature knows infinitely less of the human heart than the
simplest Christian who lives beneath the Cross of Jesus.*
—Dietrich Bonhoeffer, *Life Together*

God has given us many good rhythms in life. The rhythm of
sound is music. The rhythm of color is beauty. The rhythm
of words is poetry. But he has also given us a timeless
rhythm that is meant to be central to all of our lives,
namely the rhythm of the Christian life.

The Who, What, and When

The rhythm of the Christian life is love—directed toward
God and others. It is a biblically based, centuries-old
belief that time alone with God and time together with

others are intimately connected and work in tandem to glorify God. Our best life is no less than a life intentionally spent with God and others. It is the fullest, most satisfying way of living. This rhythm is the abundant life Jesus spoke about redeeming us for—being in a never-ending relationship with God and his people.

Regrettably, the modern Christian life has become fragmented. We have some idea, perhaps, about what individual prayer, giving, studying, and other spiritual disciplines are; but what about the rhythm that connects them all? It has become easy to drift away from love and into systematized performance focused solely on the sanctification of one individual believer, ourselves.

The moment we hear the word "rhythm" related to our spiritual life, we probably think about balancing work and rest, maintaining certain tempos in life, or perhaps liturgical practices. We think about balancing two compartmentalized aspects of the Christian life instead of infusing each aspect with the other. While all of those things are good to consider, there is still a more basic need for us to understand and take seriously: *the* rhythm of the Christian life.

This book is a first step toward drawing attention to and enlarging in practical ways the rhythm God expresses in Scripture, and that Bonhoeffer notes in *Life Together*. We cannot simply respond, "But I already attend church and spend time with God." We cannot merely say, "I am already practicing the spiritual disciplines—praying, reading, giving, serving, worshipping."

By now, we have seen that "the rhythm" is not some nebulous slot somewhere between spiritual disciplines and experiencing life seasonally. We are also not dealing with the individual muscles or bones in the body, but rather the connecting tissues and tendons and how the entire system works together in our Christian life. It is the awareness of how our daily time alone and time together relate to each other in an alternating way.

In the rhythm of the Christian life, individual desires to be served turn into Christlike desires to serve others (Mark 10:45). Individual goals and interests become secondary to the goals and interests of other believers (Phil. 2:3–4). Individual attitudes grow into joining attitudes (Heb. 10:24–25). Living in the rhythm of the Christian life means that personal prayer includes intercessory prayer for others. It means that individual Bible studies and communal Bible studies work in tandem. It means that solitude and fellowship are spiritually connected and supernaturally support each other.

Together, the two-beat rhythm of the Christian life fosters godliness, health, and love. If we do not have time alone, then we will eventually fail during our time together. If we do not have time together, then we will ultimately fail in our time alone.

How gloriously different we all are, but how perfectly and permanently united we all are in Christ, able to live in rhythm with God and each other. This timeless unity and rhythm is applicable when everything seems to take forever (childhood), or where time passes in large chunks without much warning (midlife), or when life moves at a slower pace (old age). It runs through the whole gamut of life. It is about our individual and corporate identity in Christ, who alone reconciles us with

God and each other. In Christ—and in Christ alone—the rhythm receives its redemptive value and attains its goal. The focus point of our bond is Jesus Christ, who binds us together into one family under one God. The rhythm is part of God's brilliant design, swaying between time alone and time together.

Every person made in God's image should live in the rhythm of the Christian life—experiencing the interconnectedness and reciprocal effect at play between our time together with others and our time alone with God—all the days of his or her life.

The Why

When Jesus entered the world, he said to God the Father, "Behold, I have come to do your will" (Heb. 10:9). He was given a definitive purpose and mission in coming to the world, namely "that the world might be saved through him" (John 3:17). He repeatedly tells us that the main reason he carries out and says what he does is because "the Father has commanded me" (John 14:31). Jesus's strong understanding of his purpose and what the Father commanded motivated his actions, even to the point of death on the cross.

God has also given us a clear purpose and mission. We are to glorify God by making disciples of all peoples. We accomplish this by loving God with all of our heart, mind, soul, and strength, and loving our neighbors as ourselves. This ought to be the main reason why we intentionally live in the rhythm of the Christian life. But it is not the only reason why. In fact, the never-ending presence of God and others in heaven one day gives us never-ending reasons to love God and others today. Among the reasons, we will only consider two main ones here, as well as note a few others for further consideration.

Love

As we just mentioned, the rhythm of the Christian life is rooted in love. It begins with God's love for us in Christ. We love him because he first loved us (1 John 4:19). Then, our love for him is expressed in loving others. This is grounded in the greatest commandment, which three of the four Gospels recount (Matt. 22:34–40; Mark 12:28–34; Luke 10:25–28). Jesus is asked which commandment is "the most important," but he responds with two commandments—not one. Both commandments together hold the top position. "On these two commandments depend all the law and the prophets," and are therefore the greatest. It is not one or the other but both that are critical to God's kingdom agenda.

What is more, they are tightly linked by the key verb "love." Love for God is the basis for loving our neighbor. Rhythmic Christian love in which we love God with all of our heart, soul, and mind expresses itself in loving others as we love ourselves. Love stands at the center of why we should live in the rhythm. It is the fuel for the rhythm.

In the Gospel of John, which is the only gospel that does not contain the account of the two greatest commandments, we see the same emphasis on the flow of love. Jesus states, "As the Father has loved me, so have I loved you" (15:9). Again, the subject is love. Again, we see the rhythm between an individual and his community. Jesus goes on to say that as we experience his love individually, we are also to mirror his love with others (John 15:12).

Obedience

If we love, we obey (John 14:15). We show our love by our obedience to all Jesus commanded. When we obey, we are showing an outward expression of our inward change. Jesus, Paul, and others share this connecting truth on multiple occasions. Attitudinal change and behavioral change go hand-in-hand. In Christ, we experience a transformation of our hearts *and* lives. Our obedience reveals our hearts in specific, life-related situations. We do not simply have behavior modification; we also have an internal heart transformation.

This is true if we look at our lives right now. At some point, we gained enough motivation to pursue the things we have, such as our homes, cars, clothing, spouses, or careers. We had a desire for them that grew into a willingness to act. That willingness to act evolved into obtaining the goal. There is a direct link between what we love and what we do. Our actions reveal our heart. If we love God and others, we will act accordingly. Our rhythms will show our values! Obeying God's command, then, provides another reason why we ought to live in the rhythm.

A Few Other Reasons to Live within the Rhythm

Living in this rhythm brings clarity to our Christian lives. If we have ever been confused about the Bible and how to apply it, needed clarity about God's will, desired direction regarding the various paths before us, wanted help discerning certain relationships, needed discernment for how to address certain social and ethical issues, then we have directly experienced why we need to embrace the rhythm of the Christian life. When we embrace this rhythm, we can interact with these issues communally so we are equipped to deal with them individually. We can then share our individual experiences communally so others can benefit individually.

In Christ, we were created with a purpose, and fulfilling our purpose includes spending time with God and others. This is what our godly brothers and sisters throughout history have done. Bonhoeffer was not the only one—observe the lives of Augustine, Luther, Calvin, and Edwards; Perpetua, Macrina, Katharina, and Isabella. They each lived in the rhythm. There is a real sense of empowerment living in the rhythm to which God calls us. If he calls us to it (which he does), then he will empower us to live it (which he does).

As we saw in Scripture, the best lives were those of people who lived in the rhythm. Look again at the testimonies of Moses, David, Daniel, Paul, Peter, and James. Reconsider how the elderly widow from Luke 2 remained active by nourishing her spiritual needs and proclaiming the good news to others. There is an excitement in going beyond theory to reality and experiencing what it is like to live in God's wonderful rhythm. It revives our soul. It illumines our path. It strengthens our faith.

The promise of eternal life ought to motivate us as well, especially as this life is evaporating quickly. What precious hope we have that one day we will see the face of Jesus (Rev. 22:4). We will receive the crown of life—forever enjoying a relationship with God in the fullest while we gather communally, singing praises to him (Rev. 7:9–10). This is where real, lasting beauty is found. James keeps this motivating factor in front of the recipients of his letter (James 1:12), as Paul does to the Christians in Rome (Rom. 8:18), and as Peter does to the churches in Asia Minor (1 Pet. 1:3–5).

For sure, none of us is perfect or has an ideal situation to live in—we are all temporary residents in this land of exile. But we are not alone, and we have hope because Jesus has promised to be with us to the end of the age (Matt. 28:20).

The consequences of not living in the rhythm are no less motivating. The statistics are not in our favor when we live outside of the rhythm, and the outcomes are disastrous. Consider again the testimonies of Achan, Uzziah, Ahaz, Ananias and Sapphire, Phygelus and Hermogenes, and Demas. Like these examples, we can cause our spiritual family to become weaker. We squander our gifts and talents. We miss God's blessings. We do not maximize our potential. We experience regular and noticeable pain. We drift into disobedience and sin. The stark differences between life with and without the rhythm are staggering.

In the end, there is love to express, commands to obey, a purpose to fulfill, examples to follow, promises to claim, sins to avoid, challenges to face, eternal life to anticipate. The rhythm of the Christian life is logical, intellectually. It feels right, emotionally. It works, practically.

However, it is not enough for us merely to be motivated to do it. We must do it.

The How

Many things will compete to defeat the rhythm in our lives. Even now, as we stop and look over our shoulder, we can see some of the things that are vying for our time, and if left unchecked, will throw us off balance. For instance, with the blessings of technology have come the curses of being unrhythmical. We can work in industries that require the tough work of shift work—throwing off our biological clocks. We can be on call from anywhere at any time—hindering our regular intervals of undistracted time alone. We can communicate with people we will never meet in person—preventing physical presence and authentic community.

C. S. Lewis, in his work *The Screwtape Letters*, provides us a unique perspective here. He shares how God perfectly balances our love of change and our love of permanence:

> He gives them the seasons, each season different
> yet every year the same, so that spring is always
> felt as a novelty yet always as the recurrence of
> an immemorial theme. He gives them in His
> Church a spiritual year; they change from a fast
> to a feast, but it is the same feast as before. (136)

Such rhythms are from God. But Lewis also goes on to suggest some ways by which the demonic realm tries to defeat such rhythms and make us imbalanced. They create "the demand for infinite, or unrhythmical, change kept up." They move us out of sync "by inflaming the horror of the Same Old Thing." They intensify "the desire for novelty" (137).

Indeed, Satan's activities are designed to thwart our relationship with God and others. Paul blames Satan alone for hindering his attempts with Silvanus and Timothy to see the Thessalonian church "face to face" (1 Thess. 2:18). We see in the life of Jesus that Satan is OK with our physical nourishment (Luke 4:3), worldly success (Luke 4:5–6), and even us exercising faith in God, as long as these things are pursued from the wrong motives (Luke 4:9–11). What he is not OK with is our being in rhythm with God and others.

How, then, do we do it? How do we follow God's pattern for our life and resist the devil's strategies to obstruct it? How can we possibly infuse this rhythm into our lives, especially if our life is already out of sync?

In Scripture, we see an effective plan played out in Ezra's life: "For Ezra had set his heart *to study* the Law of the LORD, and *to do it* and *to teach* his statues and rules in Israel" (Ezra 7:10; italics added). Therefore, let us get practical and intentional by following Ezra's three-fold progression.

Study It

We must start with God's word. Read and meditate on it. Examine our rhythms and the rhythm by it. Test our experiences with it—ensuring that our interactions with people are loving, our growth is increasing, our gifts are edifying the church, our light is shining before others, our teaching is accurate. Bonhoeffer writes, "It is not our heart that determines our course, but God's Word." The Psalmist tells us, "Great are the works of the LORD, studied by all who delight in them" (Ps. 111:2). Jesus quoted this passage from Deuteronomy during one of the devil's temptations, "Man shall not live by bread alone, but by every word that comes from the mouth of God" (Matt. 4:4).

This little book is not enough. At best, it is a preliminary supplement to studying God's Word. The inspired biblical accounts were written for our instruction, and they help us learn about the rhythm God designed for our life and how only Jesus can rescue us from our sin and restore us to complete harmony.

We should not just study about the rhythm but according to the rhythm. Meaning, we should not only study alone but also communally. Studying alone should certainly be a staple of our devotional life, at least for those of us blessed to live in literate societies. Yet the model of Christ, the missionary efforts of the early church, and the message of the New Testament authors all uphold corporate times of studying. As individualistic as we are, and as isolated as we are becoming, we need to seize upon more occasions and opportunities to come together and grow as communities.

Jesus, Paul, and the earliest Christian communities all read communally (Luke 4:16–30; Acts 17:1–3). Indeed, the New Testament documents were written with the intention of being read in community. Paul explicitly instructed some of his letters to be read aloud (Col. 4:16; 1 Thess. 5:27), along with other Scripture (1 Tim. 4:13).

Reading and studying together counters our individualistic tendencies and fosters humility and gratitude. By discussing Scripture in community, we acknowledge our inability to fully grasp God's truth on our own, and we learn to appreciate the insights of others. Gifts are shared, weaknesses offset, and personal interpretations exposed to inquiry. When we receive God's revelation together and interact with one another, our personal biases are exposed, and other opinions are conveyed and considered. This teaches us to listen attentively, think carefully, question kindly, and respond humbly. Our souls are formed when we study together, as well as when we search Scripture daily on our own.

Studying alone fosters studying together, and studying together fosters studying alone. Such is every aspect of the rhythm of the Christian life.

Do It

As life pulls us this way and that, as we are constantly juggling relationships and responsibilities, now is the time for us to (re)calibrate our lives (2 Cor. 6:2; Heb. 3:15; Rev. 3:11). We must prayerfully come up with a plan and, with God's grace, execute it.

Although an algorithm for the rhythm does not exist, we must develop a rhythm mindset while living in the rhythm. We must remind ourselves that our time alone is not merely about us alone, and that our time together is not only about the gathered community. As we become more or less godly, our community does as well. As our church community weakens or strengthens, we do too.

As our minds grasp the rhythm, we must live it out in our lives. To do nothing is to submit to the powers of this age. We must live and experience the rhythm, not just read and talk about it. We must practice it, not just profess it. As individuals in community, we are like the binary stars that astronomers have discovered in deep space. These stars are locked into a mutual orbit around each other, bound together by their separate gravities in a rhythmic round dance of mutual dependence.

The hallmarks of accomplishing almost anything in life include creating a reasonable game plan, being intentionally committed, and acquiring appropriate accountability. Those common characteristics are no less necessary in the Christian life, but there is much more to consider regarding "the rhythm" as opposed to "rhythms" in general. That is why we are not discussing the ins and outs of time alone or time together. Rather, we are focusing on some of the best practices for cultivating the back-and-forth rhythm and for living with the rhythm mindset.

First, do not focus on creating goals. This is not a box to be checked. Instead, establish patterns—patterns that help you live in the rhythm. Set and follow segmented time frames. Perhaps a sleeping schedule of 9:30 p.m. to 5:30 a.m., followed by a time alone with God between 5:30 a.m. and 6:30 a.m., which then leads into time together with others throughout the day. Arranging and observing daily, weekly, monthly, and yearly periods of both time alone with God and time together with others is essential. When exactly is the best time to do them? It depends on each person's circumstances, but probably when you are the most physically alert and mentally aware. Start there.

Whatever our patterns become, we must craft habits according to the rhythm. We must keep up this practice with great care and watchfulness. Otherwise, we will find ourselves out of balance.

Occasionally, we are susceptible to neglecting the rhythm altogether. When parents forget the rhythm, they get stuck in the rut of chores, correcting children, and transporting between activities. When people in old age forget the rhythm, they get hung up on physical decline, social losses, and financial security. Even though life circumstances will change significantly as we advance in life, the rhythm should not. We must spend time alone with God and others regularly, indeed rhythmically. This will ensure that a parent's time alone with God is put to use in how she corrects her children, or the conversations he initiates during the drive to band practice or a sporting event. An elderly person will see how their time together with others strengthens their time alone so it can be filled with joy instead of loneliness.

During times when life disrupts our established schedule, we can still maintain the rhythm. Even when our plate is full, our margin is thin, and life feels overwhelming, we can still find a way to stay faithful.

To make sure the rhythm remains firmly established in our life, even when the pace of life changes, we might need to modify our established routine temporarily. Just as we may shorten our fitness training when time is limited, or opt for an at-home workout instead of our normal gym activity, our full spiritual routine becomes a partial one. Our one hour of time alone changes to ten, twenty, or thirty minutes as an interim measure. Our thirty minutes of concerted prayer turns into just being able to lift up a few brief prayers in the short term. Our extended time of meditation at home becomes quiet reflections and introspection on the commute to work for the time being—turning off our radio, podcast, or phone.

Interfering times that seem quite unmanageable hit us all, but adapting with some provisional measures helps us safeguard the rhythm in our life.

We must remember, however, that we are susceptible to spiritual weakening when we do this. We need to be careful that an initial departure does not become a final departure. It may become all too easy to allow the momentary change or subtle pattern shift to become permanent; then complacency sets in. From there, it only gets worse. During such spiritual maneuvering, it is relatively effortless to drift from our earlier commitment to God. Our diminishing time will continue to diminish until it is demolished. The initial switch swiftly becomes disobedience or the new norm. During such times, we ought to recall the words of our precious Savior: "apart from me you can do nothing" (John 15:5).

Living in the rhythm is more than just performing some spiritual activities consistently. It is not until we rightly remember others during our time alone, or apply our time alone to our time together, that we are "doing it." Despite the differences between them, we must experience the interconnectedness and reciprocal effect at play between our time together with others and our time alone with God.

After we pray for someone's sickness, we should go visit him or her. After we visit the sick, we should go pray for them. After we study the Word, we ought to counsel and strengthen someone accordingly. After we receive the Word communally, we should go back to search Scripture individually. After we have taken the log out of our eye, we must still go to our brother or sister and help them with the splinter that is in their eye. After someone helps us with the splinter in our eye, we should bring it to the Lord and repent.

In everything we do, we must glorify God and consider our brothers and sisters in Christ. We must gauge our souls before God and others. We must recognize our thought patterns and ask ourselves hard questions to uncover our motives. Are our thoughts largely others-focused, or mostly self-focused? What is the state of our soul right now, and who else knows and cares about it? Who is helping us endure to the end? Do we take the commands in passages like Hebrews 3:13 seriously, and determine ways we can "exhort one another every day" in our context? Are we imitating Jesus, who was in the habit of spending time alone with God, or are we like the Pharisees doing everything to be seen by man (Matt. 23:5)?

We should not attend a local church merely to have time together or be blessed, but to serve one another. When we attend for the sole purpose of our individual spiritual growth, or our individual social time, or our individual building up, we approach God in a selfish manner and weaken the body of Christ. The church body needs all we can offer. Let's identify a few people and plan time to get together frequently. Invite a few people into our life that will enhance the rhythm in our life and who we can serve also. Intentionally form the kind of life together that makes the rhythm a fact and not a fantasy.

Whatever we do, we must pray and take action. We must determine where we fall on the spectrum of

Bonhoeffer's danger zones: "Let him who cannot be alone beware of community. Let him who is not in community beware of being alone" (*Life Together*, 78). We must consider all that is taking away from living in the rhythm right now and realize the dangers that await us if we live outside the rhythm. Whatever time alone and time together look like in our context, it should never develop independently or at the expense of the local church community. We must grow together, hand in hand, in the context of a church community.

We must take heed. Satan will envy our happiness and is seeking to destroy our lives (1 Pet. 5:8). We must pay attention to the rhythms in our life and become wise stewards of our time (Eph. 5:15–16). Live in sync with the rhythm of the Christian life. Let go of unrealistic expectations. Seize opportunities to increase genuine fellowship and reduce isolation. Keep eternity in view.

In light of everything I have pointed out, let's consider just a few more ways we can ensure we live in the rhythm of the Christian life. We could:

- Take control of our appointment calendar
- Carve out short periods in our already established schedule, such as cutting our thirty-minute or one hour lunch down to twenty or forty-five minutes so that we can use it for spiritual development
- Re-center our focus throughout the day by lifting up prayers at specific hours, like 9 a.m., 12 p.m., and 3 p.m.
- Schedule more mealtime fellowship

- Seek out help from our pastor, or some other mature believer
- Link up with someone from church if we do not have immediate family around us
- Go over to someone's house who knows how to live in the rhythm if we do not know where or how to start doing these things—and if it is our house that people come to, we could follow up with them regularly
- Let others—spouse, coworker, community— know about our routine for accountability
- Start taking notes of what God is doing over time
- Record and share things throughout the day and week that can be catalysts for maintaining the rhythm
- Make sure we read at least one Psalm and one Proverb every day—the Psalms frequently depict a person's time alone with God, while the Proverbs regularly relate to our time together with others
- Add some visual reminders to our life, like putting a globe or displaying a world map some-where as a reminder to pray for our persecuted family worldwide; putting pictures on our fridge of missionaries we support; posting Scripture around our house; bringing index cards with Bible verses in our car for memorization
- Always have a Bible or other edifying literature nearby or with us, especially during expected wait times—at the doctor's office, in security lines

when traveling, or while someone else is getting ready

- Attach spiritual exercises to our daily routines—perhaps during our morning ritual, we could pray through our prayer list while brushing our teeth, putting on makeup, or getting dressed
- Come up with an alternative plan if we are unable to keep up with the pace of our current ones, like reading our entire Bible in a year. Do it in two or three years if needed—just make sure you engage Scripture daily.

The main point in all this is that God calls us to live in the rhythm of time alone with him and time together with others. This rhythm should be as regular as eating, drinking, and bathing. If we do not bathe or brush our teeth for a day or so, we will not die because of it. But the longer we go without performing such daily activities, the worse it is for us and everyone around us.

The same relates to our spiritual hygiene. If we ever miss a day or two, we must be swift to shift our attention back to where it belongs: on the rhythm between God and others. We ought to do whatever it takes to stay in the rhythm of the Christian life for our health and the health of our community. The rhythm keeps us in the epicenter of our spiritual life.

Teach It

By studying about and living in the rhythm, we ought to realize that it is not just for us. We do not hide how God moves in our lives. We proclaim it to others, just as the

Psalmist says, "I have not hidden your deliverance within my heart; I have spoken of your faithfulness and your salvation; I have not concealed your steadfast love and your faithfulness from the great congregation" (Ps. 40:10).

We are commanded to ask for wisdom. When we receive it, it is not merely for self-improvement. Peter tells us that Paul wrote to others according to the wisdom given to him (2 Pet. 3:15; cf. 1 Cor. 12:8). What Paul received from the Lord, he gave to others (1 Cor. 11:23). Jesus called the twelve disciples to himself in order to send them out to teach others (Mark 3:14). What Timothy heard from Paul, he was commanded to pass on to others (2 Tim. 2:2). Jude was "eager to write" to others about the salvation we share and "compelled to write and urge" them to contend for the faith (Jude 3). In a similar way, we are to share.

Opportunities to teach others are not restricted to sacred spaces. Philip taught from Isaiah in a chariot. Paul read God's Word in synagogues, taught it in lecture halls, and evangelized with it along riverbanks and in market-places. One way early Christians loved their neighbors was by reading, teaching, and discussing God's truth with them. In fact, our lives are meant to be a walking letter for everyone to examine and read (2 Cor. 3:2–3).

We must maximize our opportunities to teach and encourage others. Sunday school, home Bible studies, or other face-to-face meetings throughout the week provide ample opportunities for us to teach and show others how to live in the rhythm God intended, while encouraging them to keep their loves and priorities straight. Whatever the context, we must pass along God's truth to others.

But what is it that still hinders so many people from doing all this?

Excuses

Even when we believe the truth, understand the value, and see the results, we do not always make it a priority or follow through with a commitment. When we do not apply it to our lives, excuses abound. We try to rationalize things in our minds: *My relationship with God is private. I am too busy. I cannot find the right community. I have nothing to contribute. I am not equipped or ready. I do not want anyone to know about my personal life. I will just be rejected.*

Granted, it can be disturbing and frightening to venture out far from our regularly traveled and well-established paths marked by our own fears, traditions, preferences, and biases. We can convince ourselves of just about anything, especially when it involves getting up, going out, and doing something: "The sluggard says, 'There is a lion in the road! There is a lion in the streets!'" (Prov. 26:13). But most of the so-called reasons and inconveniences are just emotional or imaginative things in our minds. The root problem, as we have seen already, seems to be a lack of trust in God.

The rhythm of the Christian life is medicine for our soul: spending time with God and others. It is about experiencing the "already/not yet" of God's kingdom. Believers are "already" experiencing some of the blessings of and taking part in the kingdom of God but "not yet" in its fullness. The problem is, many people are looking for the "not yet" part, while missing the "already" aspect.

A FINAL APPEAL

Throughout this work, we have sought to explore the rhythm of the Christian life: the harmonious flow and strong connection between our time alone with God and time spent with one another. We have seen that the rhythm of the Christian life is not another fad, or something we master, or merely a good idea to consider. It is foundational to our life as believers in Christ. God the Father commanded it. God the Son modeled it. God the Holy Spirit preserves it. The greatest commandment reveals it. The biblical authors proclaimed it. The early church embraced it. We are the ones responsible for it.

Consider again some of the things we gleaned. There is a reason why Scripture makes it clear that we are to do everything for God's glory *and* the benefit of others. There is a reason why it was Jesus's custom to pray to God individually *and* gather in the synagogue communally. There is a reason why Jesus calls us to himself *and* sends out to others. There is a reason why Satan thwarts our relationship with God *and* others. There is a reason why we are commanded to focus on Christ *and* others. There is a reason why Paul aims to win Christ's approval *and* human acceptance for the advance of the gospel. There is a reason why Jesus answered "*the* greatest commandment" question with two commandments. There is a reason why Paul tells us that the proper kingdom focus *combines* pleasing God with being acceptable to people. There is a reason why specific metaphors, like parts of a body or stones of a building, exist in Scripture. There is a reason why singular *and* plural pronouns are at times interchangeable in the same context in Scripture. There is a reason why people fail when they are not in community or cannot be alone. There is a reason why people succeed when they do both.

The reason is that God ordained a specific rhythm for us to live in. We are calling it the rhythm of the Christian life.

If either aspect of the rhythm God ordained seems uninteresting, or if the overall rhythm seems too costly, we have not fully grasped or embraced God's purpose for our life. Finding any rhythm (let alone living in *the* rhythm) is difficult, nay impossible apart from Christ. The rhythm itself demonstrates how our Christian lives are oriented in a radically new way toward loving God and others. Our Christian life and experience is much deeper and richer than our life before Christ.

In this book, we saw people and communities live happier, godlier, and more productive lives because they lived in the rhythm. We saw others who lived miserable, evil, and wasteful lives because they lived out of sync with God's rhythm. It was not just about having private, family, and corporate times, but how they connected. Individuals and communities are strongest when they live in the rhythm of the Christian life. It is the center of gravity.

We not only live in the rhythm of the Christian life, but, with God's grace, we pass it along to the generations that follow us because they saw us living it and heard us teaching it. As the Psalmist says, "Let this be recorded for a generation to come, so that a people yet to be created may praise the LORD" (Ps. 102:18; cf. Ps. 145:4). We, too, must maintain a proper perspective by connecting the rhythm with the future. We, too, must do what we can—fulfilling our calling to ensure God's renown lasts.

Allowing the rhythm to regulate our lives will ensure that we never waste them. We cannot go back and change what has already happened, but we can start over and change the direction we are heading. There is no better way to follow Jesus on the narrow path of faithfulness in all seasons of our lives than to live in the rhythm of the Christian life.